The Mountain World

THE MOUNTAIN WORLD

by Curtis W. Casewit

A Ridge Press Book | Random House

Editor-in-Chief: Jerry Mason
Editor: Adolph Suehsdorf
Art Director: Albert Squillace
Associate Editor: Ronne Peltzman
Associate Editor: Joan Fisher
Art Associate: David Namias
Art Production: Doris Mullane
Picture Research: Marion Geisinger

Library of Congress Cataloging in Publication Data
Casewit, Curtis W
   The mountain world.

   1. Mountains—Pictorial works. I. Title.
GB511.C37   910'.031'43   76-12542
ISBN 0-394-40094-1

Printed in Italy by Mondadori Editore, Verona.

Jacket: (front) Galen A. Rowell; (back) British Columbia
Department of Travel & Industry.

Contents

Introduction

I have lived much of my life among mountains. I acknowledge the plains, the prairies, the level spaces and flatlands of this world, but it is for the high elevations that I have the most admiration and the greatest affinity. Much of *The Mountain World* is testimony to my enthusiasm. The world of mountains is of the widest interest and diversity, offers many challenges, and often presents us with extraordinary natural beauty. I hope my perspectives are reasonably fresh; I have tried not to be too rapturous, although that is not easily done.

Most fascinating, I think, is our changing knowledge of mountains, in particular our relatively recent recognition of their mortality. Symbols of permanence, immutable, seemingly everlasting? True. But mountains do in fact wax and wane, we now learn, like all earthly things. Several of the great ranges have risen and fallen several times in the span of geologic time. The Appalachians are extremely old, the Himalayas youthful giants not yet fully grown.

The processes of mountain formation are several and continuous: erosion, volcanic eruption, and crustal fracturing, folding, and overlapping. Geophysicists currently tend to believe that displacements of the crust are the result of collisions between tectonic plates—that the Indian plate, for instance, strains powerfully against the Asian land mass. The resulting crunch buckles the earth into accordion pleats whose high points are Himalayan mountains. Plates whose edges have been overridden are melted in the fiery furnaces of the earth's interior and replenish the sea of molten magma on which all tectonic plates float.

All this is discussed farther on. I mention it here because we know that the geology and, for that matter, the ecology of mountains bear as importantly on the future of the mountain world as its ski resorts.

The latter, of course, have had vast economic impact on somnolent mountain villages previously content with a life of *milch* cows and cheese. For the past thirty or forty years the universal affection for skiing has been remaking old—even ancient—mountain communities as well as establishing new ones with their hotels, lifts, express highways, airports, and imported fashions, architecture, sports, and life styles.

In the 1970s this has resulted in a curiously mixed mountain society, an ambience in which work and play combine or, more likely, coexist, each independent of the other. For while mountains now are year-round enterprises, attracting summertime artists, music-lovers, and intellectual conference-goers as readily as campers, backpackers, dudes, climbers, and winter skiers, still the local people remain. Many earn their livelihood by providing goods and services for the pilgrims, but many more continue in the old ways, farming and herding as they have always done.

Between these early settlers and the new ones, there is another generation —engineers, mechanics, foresters, miners, rangers, scientists, and all the rest whose talents or inclinations or professions have brought them to the mountain to change its contours, risk its hazards, drive its tunnels, erect its dams, gut its wealth, reap its resources, guard its frontiers, and perhaps preserve it for further use and enjoyment.

However mankind may try to alter the mountains, there is an elaborate and wonderful natural environment already established on the heights. This is a fundamental part of the mountain world, worthy of cultivation and respect.

The Mountain World would have been difficult to write without the help of a great many people who made suggestions and read parts of the manuscript. Others assisted with research or shared some of their mountain experiences with me.

There is not enough space to name everyone. My heartfelt thanks go to Dr. Michael C. Grant, director of the Mountain Research Station, Institute of Arctic and Alpine Research; Dr. Richard Pearl, professor of geology; Dr. Thomas M. Griffiths, geologist and world traveler; Clayton Freiheit, zoologist; Charles Robinson, tunnel engineer; Norman Ford, author and adventurer; Dr. Maury Travis, geomorphologist; Bill Forrest, elite climber and designer of climbing equipment; Bob Akins, naturalist; and Wilhelm Neu, Hilde Schmidt, Rebecca Kast, John Zukosky, Max Galambos, June Bates, Karen Kaehny, Barbara Johnson, Helen Gaynor, Pat Gish, Doug Perry, M. Pabst, David Grotewohl, and W. R. Koger.

C.C.
Denver, Colorado

1

The Mountains

*Preceding pages: Snow
complicates ascent for roped
climbers on slope of Mont
Blanc, Europe's highest
peak, on French-Italian border.
Above: Thickly wooded San
Juans of southwestern Colorado
are near termination of
great Rockies system.*

12

The Alps loom ahead, snow-whitened battlements, convoluted, labyrinthine, and impassive, as you drive north through Italy or south in West Germany. Similarly, on a good day, pointed down an arrow-straight highway through the corn, you can see the Rockies from the western borders of Kansas and Nebraska. The wavy blue-gray line on the horizon grows and sharpens as you near Colorado; by the time you reach Denver the Continental Divide is all gleam and sheen. Other mountains dominate more limited space. The Tetons, massive yet self-contained, are stunning in their angularity, their abrupt upward thrust out of the Wyoming plains. And others are singular. The Matterhorn, though it stands in a cluster of Alpine peaks, commands the eye. Should your first glimpse of the monolith occur as the peak emerges from cloud cover in clearing weather, it is difficult to repress a gasp.

The greatness of mountains is dazzling, evocative, awesome. In humankind the pangs felt in the presence of mountainous visions may be felt for a lifetime. "Mountains," wrote an English climber, "move us in some way which nothing else does. The feeling is so deep, so pure, so personal as to be almost sacred, and too intimate for ordinary mention. . . ."

Strong words these, yet incontrovertible for anyone who has stood before an Annapurna, a Mount McKinley, or an Eiger. One summer I rented a small chalet across from the Eiger's formidable north face. There was work to do and I came alone. But I found it difficult to concentrate. The Ogre kept drawing me to the window or onto the balcony to gaze at its vast shape, at its six thousand feet of adamantine verticality that blocked the sun and left me only a wedge of sky. At night my sleep was interrupted by the deep rumbles of stone avalanches. In daytime I saw blocks of ice suddenly shear off the perpendicular face and crash, after a ponderous long fall, into the valley below. Or tons of snow with an uneasy purchase on one of the mountain's steep facets would suddenly let go, slide thunderously, and cascade into space. Water could be seen pouring down couloirs between overhangs and spurting from the titan's face. Even on the immutable Eiger, gravity and the forces of erosion ceaselessly work, and in the vigor of his responses the giant seems alive.

Of course, this manner of describing mountains is age-old. Mountains are truly impressive and humanity has projected the full range of its feelings—as well as of its vocabulary—upon them. It has regarded them with reverence and also with fear. It has lived among them, accepting their blessings, yet always considered ascents in terms of conquest.

For the reverent, height and elevation have been associated since earliest times with divinity. Imagination has assigned ethereal spaces as godly abodes, and the apex of mountains as hallowed regions from which to offer homage.

History and legend are replete with sacred mountains. Homer and Hesiod sing of Mount Olympus as the home of Zeus

*Air view of Alps
(above) shows
severe compression
of land mass.
Forbidding north
wall of Eiger
(r) is a Class VI
climb. Opposite:
Placid uplands
of South Tyrol.*

14

Sinai Wilderness: No one knows which mountain Moses ascended to receive the Commandments, but it probably was one of the Gebel Musa range, rising amid a desert heated by sun and controversy since Pharaohs first mined its copper.

and the Olympian gods, who were shrouded from the sight of men by clouds eternally wreathing the summit. In fact, although it is the highest point in Greece, Olympus is a mere 9,570 feet (2,917 m), and Parnassus, above Delphi, consecrated to Apollo and the Muses, is 8,000.

On Mount Ararat, in Turkey, Noah's Ark descended, on Mount Sinai Moses received the Commandments. Serene, symmetrical Fujiyama is ascended by countless pilgrims. Mighty Everest is revered by the Sherpa guides of Nepal, and Tibet's theocracy dwells in the rarefied spiritual and temporal atmosphere of the furthest Himalayan ranges.

The heights may also harbor evil or manifestations of the supernatural. It has never been hard for the fervid imaginations of simple folk to find hair-raising explanations for the inexplicable: the creaks and groans and sudden crashes of the living mountain, the echoing peals of mountain thunder, the lightning bolts of an electrical storm playing fitfully about a summit. From here it is a short step to a witches' Sabbath on Bald Mountain, to the frenzy of Scandinavian trolls in the hall of a mountain king, to a game of bowls and an amnesiac sleep in the Catskills, to dragons, Valkyries, and to dwarfs deep in mountain interiors, mining gold and crafting it into talismans.

Even much of mountain history has the quality of myth. Mountain passes —paths through the maze, doorways to stran-

gers' land beyond—have figured in some of the great adventures of history: Alexander the Great finding India through the Hindu Kush, Hannibal and his war elephants falling on the Roman rear after a daring march through the Alps, the notes of the dying Roland's horn summoning his liege Charlemagne in the Pyreneean pass at Roncesvalles.

At Peshawar, just below the Khyber Pass, where garrisons of Kipling's day guarded what British India called the North-West Frontier Province, Moslem Pathans sniped from the rocky cover of the sun-baked mountainsides. And British soldiers bound for the latrine learned to take a different route coming back from that they took going. Going gave the patient marksmen the range, coming triggered the fatal shot.

More than a century ago, John Muir, naturalist, conservationist, and wanderer of California's woods and mountains, suggested that one should go to the mountains for "their good tidings." Cares, he said, will "drop off like autumn leaves."

17

Glory of the North American West is the complex Rocky Mountain system running from Alaska to New Mexico. Pack train (l) treads carpet of wildflowers against backdrop of Canadian Rockies. Below: Stand of quaking aspen shimmers in foothills of Wyoming's Teton Range.

19

I was born in southern Germany. As a young man I hiked through the Austrian province of Carinthia with a local girl for a guide. The two of us walked up the greenest Alpine meadows. We rested above the bluest imaginable lakes. We explored the *Kärntner* villages, each with a white church and an onion steeple. The Austrian mountains proved an ideal setting for experiencing the twin wonders of youth and love. We philosophized on many a trail.

It was thirty years before I got back to this scenic Carinthian land, to the well-tended fields, the neat houses with their geraniums, the old drinking fountains. Carinthia's white steeples—some dating to the twelfth and thirteenth centuries—still blended into the landscape. During the last lap of a hike, a modest medieval church drew my attention. It occupied the highest spot in the village. The façade was humble enough. But above the hand-carved door, a wooden sign summed up some important thoughts: "*Geh' hinauf in die Berge,*" it read. "Go up into the mountains." "*Deine Seele braucht es. Und dein Körper auch.*" "Your soul needs it. And your body, too."

It is true that the melody of a brook, or trails bordered by wild forget-me-nots, ferns, and daisies soothe the soul, that every stride through the gently undulating Austrian countryside enhances the benefits of exercise. The sun caresses the wanderer's face. The blood sings. At such moments, it is easy to enjoy the high country.

To millions of recreational skiers, white slopes are the be-all and end-all of the mountain world. The seasoned skier demands long *pistes*, the longer the better. I vividly recall the morning I skied down a live French glacier for about eighteen weaving kilometers. It was routine to my guide, but—ah!—on my tongue how sweet the taste of adventure! That brilliant spring day we skirted a series of crevasses, a waterfall, frozen lakes, chunky Alpine trees. It took me all morning to reach the valley.

A mountain activist will also hear the call from the ice fields of Washington State. A climber ascends a glacier with crampons—metal spikes—strapped under his feet. (Watch them! The metal can tear holes in the tyro's corduroy pants.) Sweat stings the forehead. The rope bites into the waist. But always up, up, up, behind the guide. One summer I joined a group of hikers bound for a 14,000-footer. Ambitious leadership! The brute had to be done in six instead of ten hours. It took me twelve, with leg-buckling results. There was nothing left to drink, and I struggled back into camp, lips and throat stiff from dehydration. Finally, I quenched my thirst, crawled into the tent, and was asleep in thirty seconds. Muscle pains the next day reminded me of my ordeal, and my kneecaps burned for a week. But I had no regrets.

Such mountain-inflicted tortures may be antidotes for the life of the city. A New York stockbroker spends all his free time locked in struggles against rugged peaks over 10,000 feet—one man's reaction to an age of affluence. "All of us need to push ourselves a little," he says, "so that we can discover our limits." To increase the difficulties, ambitious mountaineers reverse the seasons, attacking the tough peaks in winter, while expert skiers try far-flung and difficult slopes in summer.

The mountain world in spring attracts other categories of visitors. Kayakers, rafters, canoeists—and rainbow trout—all come alive. In the North American West, horseback riders set out from dude ranches. On any given summer day someone visits the high country on the back of a burro or a pony, or in the saddle of a bicycle. One can run after butterflies at high elevations or seek out elusive animals with binoculars or camera.

Some come to pick wild berries, search the hillsides for rocks and minerals, sift rivers for gold, go underground in caves. Painters try to capture a pinnacle's contours—a considerable task! One minute the tints may be subtle shades of apricot, the most delicate olive, the thinnest outlines. The next moment beams and bundles of light alter the palette. A riot of greens now mingle with the strong reds, yellows, and violets of summer flora.

Many early visitors to high country where scientists and naturalists. Enos Mills, whose special interest was the Colorado Rockies, went up into the mountains because he wanted to track bears, hunt fossils, observe beavers, and "watch storms where they roar the loudest." John Muir, patient wanderer of the Sierras, wrote: "The mountains are calling and I must go."

The sun rises behind my Colorado hilltop home. A few miles away the wooded slopes are bathed in morning light. I can observe the sun's progress on Pikes Peak, at first a triangle in various shades of blue, then translucent like a glass of white wine, later still steel gray under the onslaught of an afternoon thunderstorm. The clouds press down and cover the peak's brow, nose, neck, shoulders, chest. Black curtain of rain! Then, as the day wanes, an incandescent peak once more.

In the day's last blast of sunlight, mountains glow like hot coals—what Alpine people call *Alpen-glühen*—a phenomenon caused by the sun's intensity at high altitudes. In the absence of dust particles the air reflects more light.

Climatologists can explain the changeable mountain weather. They walk for a few hours among the shifting mists of the Scottish Highlands under a milky sky which leaves a soft wetness on the skin. Suddenly, the Highlands appear once more. Clear horizon! The sun suffuses the birch forests, lights up the purple heather, brightens the lochs and braes; similarly among the rocky buttresses of Skye and the idyllic prominences of Wales. A change of weather and coloring by the hour!

Each continent has its own surprises. The traveler must prepare for an encounter with Africa's high peaks. Hemingway described one of them: "And there, ahead, as wide as all the world, great, high, and unbelievably white in the sun, was the square top of Kilimanjaro!"

21

Washington's Mount Rainier (r) and California's Shasta are volcanic peaks of America's Cascade Range, an extension of the Sierra Nevada (above). These mountains intercept eastbound rains, which irrigate coastal farms and orchards, while leaving east slopes generally arid.

An improbable setting. Mount Kilimanjaro soars 19,340 feet (5,895 m) above beige-and-gold plains, hugging a land of acacias, fertile farm fields, and bamboo forests that shelter monkeys and leopards. The mountain has been commercialized since Hemingway's day. International tourists sign up en masse for a guided journey complete with porters who set up real beds for the bivouacs. Some two hundred miles from Kilimanjaro, 17,040-foot (5,194-m) Mount Kenya soars from plains enhanced by rare animals and exotic trees.

A skier's pause on a terrace above Wengen brings him face to face with Switzerland's most sublime mountainscape—the Bernese Oberland.

"And roll the sheeted silver's waving column o'er the crag's headlong perpendicular," wrote Byron, after he lodged in Lauterbrunnen, at the foot of the Oberland's Eiger, Mönch, and Jungfrau. And in "Manfred" survive the poet's impressions of his walk on an Alpine glacier:

> O'er the savage sea,
> The glassy ocean of the mountain ice,
> We skim its rugged breakers, which put on
> The aspect of a tumbling tempest's foam,
> Frozen in a moment.

The Manx poet T. W. Brown, after watching the Jungfrau through the "bright, sweet air," wrote that she "has such moods, such unutterable smiles, such unscrutable sulks, such crowns of stars. . . ." And when John Ruskin, the English essayist, saw these Alps for the first time, he exclaimed, "Infinitely beyond all I had ever thought or dreamed!" Later he wrote that these mountains were "the beginning and the end of all natural scenery" and that to him "nothing else existed."

The Jungfrau is also of interest to less romantic sightseers. The Maiden has her own train which tunnels through parts of the Eiger, through the Mönch, and exits onto a white Jungfrau shoulder. Here is Europe's highest railroad station, and you'll even find a hotel on the Jungfraujoch.

Yet mountains also leave some people unmoved. I once spoke with an Oregon rancher whose home stood amid some of the more magnificent landscapes I'd ever seen. A spectacular hunk of the Pacific Northwest was visible through his picture windows. But the man merely shrugged. "Them Cascades mean nothin' to me," he said. "I lost nothin' up there!" The Oregon rain had ceased that morning. A new day illuminated the triangular Coast Range and highlighted giant fir trees. The shining tops marched uphill in formation. The rancher saw only bleakness. He showed no curiosity about the Cascade Kingdom, which extends for some seven hundred miles and includes Mount Adams, Mount Shasta, and Mount Rainier. The rancher hadn't been close to any of these peaks. He made his living in a lush country, but it didn't touch him.

I had just been on Mount Rainier. One gets the feel of its immensity by walking uphill through dark Washington forests of fir and spruce, hemlock and cedar, then through meadows with blooming wildflowers, while Rainier looms over all. We slept on narrow cots in a stone shelter. I still remember the nights at 10,000 feet. A mysterious wind stroked the ice banks, the roof, the window sills. The shelter had no glass panes and I could sometimes see the stars standing out with incredible sharpness. The galaxies seemed as close as the hut's lantern. The wake-up call came long before dawn. "Come on, you fellows!" the guide shouted. "Get ready!" It took time to shed the layers of sleep, to get one's head together to begin the Rainier day. It was still dark in the stone shelter. Now a lighted wick. Paper cups of bad coffee. A first bite of food. Then a look at glacier and sky, both touched by faint amber.

It always took ten minutes to get laced and roped up at Camp Muir. The guide knew about city people; he granted us enough time to absorb the dazzling views. Mountains all around. Huge, shimmering ice fields punctuated by rock. Glacial precipices. Crevasses in abundance. This meant we had to be tied to one another. We learned to walk in rhythm, so that the rope did not bite into the next person's stomach. Silence, except for the click of steel crampons on ice. The group wastes few words. Mount Rainier is primitive enough. It inspires awareness that humans are vulnerable. The party moves in unison, cautious, alert, ears cocked. The guide probes the ice for unsafe snow bridges and cornices that might conceal chasms. The first man on the rope listens carefully to every sound. When he comes to an icy fissure the decision to jump across or go around is his. One can sometimes leap a crevasse, but the ax must be held at the ready. It was exciting. I felt a thrill walking alongside the deep void. The mysterious hues of blue and green made my spine tingle. I was grateful for the presence of a capable leader, grateful for the contact with a large glacier, grateful for the vistas. Unlike the Oregon rancher, I wanted very much to be up there.

Summer months can be a delight in the Rockies. The less-visited elevations —those of Idaho and Montana—may be the most satisfying. One can backpack into Idaho's wrinkled Sawtooths for remote trails, big rocks for cragsmen, wild Alpine lakes amply stocked with fish. The Lost River Range includes Mount Borah, Idaho's highest, named for the state's powerful Senator of the thirties. Here one is far away from the back-to-back condominiums of Sun Valley. The Rockies are suitably underpopulated and unvisited. In certain sections of Colorado, too. Soaring elevations! Choose among fifty-four peaks of over 14,000 feet and, believe it or not, eleven hundred that exceed 10,000 feet. Many of these pinnacles get little business from climbers or hikers and none from tourists. One can still find serenity in the southern part of the state. The names recall the Spaniards who came in the sixteenth century to look for gold. The San Juans and the Sangre de Cristos, named perhaps by conquistadors for whom the peaks bathed in the red light of sunset symbolically resembled the blood of Christ. The range has some forty-two peaks exceeding 13,000 feet. Thin air. Flatlanders should take it

25

Opposite: Nepalese village, itself two miles high, nestles at base of Dhaulagiri, a Himalayan giant of 26,810 ft (8,172 m). Above: Serene Glencoe overlooks site of historic Scottish massacre. Kilimanjaro (l), in Tanzania, is actually two peaks. Mount Kibo, at 19,340 ft (5,895 m), is tallest in Africa.

easy at first.

From Denver, the most visible "fourteener" is Mount Evans, with another automobile road to the summit concession stands. Longs Peak, 14,256 feet (4,345 m), looks different from every direction. It serves elite climbers (who aim for the perpendicular 2,500-foot "Diamond") and hikers with enough stamina for seven to ten hours of walking. Longs' sudden thunderstorms are justly famous. The open spaces above timberline offer little protection against lightning.

The 430-mile Sierra Nevadas, or "the Great Snowy Range," as the Spaniards called them, must be considered a separate chain. The Sierras soar to their highest point at 14,495-foot (4,418-m) Mount Whitney, which also happens to be the highest peak in the United States. European travelers heap praise on Yosemite's assortment of rock domes, arched thrones, precipices, battlements. (El Capitan is an elite climbers' paradise.) John Muir devoted much of his life to this area of California, examining, studying, cataloguing, simply admiring the landscape. "A most noble rock," he wrote about one Yosemite favorite. "It seems full of thought, clothed with living light, no sense of dead stone about it . . . steadfast in serene strength like a god."

By Western standards, the ancient, glacier-worn mountains of the British Isles are humble heights, but they serve people well enough. Loftiest is 4,406-foot (1,343-m) Ben Nevis, in Scotland. But what splendid

29

*Matterhorn, one of the world's
most impressive mountains, towers over
Swiss-Italian border, near Zermatt.
It was among the first great challenges to
climbers, was finally topped in 1865.*

rock climbing there is in the Highlands, with ample terrains for hikers or "hill walkers" besides. The English Midlands and Wales abound in opportunities for rambles across the hillsides. Space? The Pennine Way extends for a respectable 250 miles, connecting Derbyshire with the distant Cheviot Hills of Scotland. In between, there are curvy paths across 2,000-foot elevations and down into flowered valleys. The Pennine Way's villages have poetic names like Windy Gyle, and the hill walker can sleep in strategically located little inns with pubs.

Certainly, western Europeans have always known how to enjoy the Alps, too. The mighty chain extends from the Mediterranean's Ligurian Sea to the Adriatic, from the valleys of Yugoslavia to the plains of France, from Vienna, Austria, to Turin, Italy. Europeans flock to inns that cling to the steep, meadowed valleys of the Austrian Arlberg. They may own chalets in the Swiss Engadine, or shuttle to Merano or Bolzano or Cortina in the Italian Alps for a yearly vacation. The vistas differ. The photogenic Dolomites are serrated, pillared, and spired. Austria's Grossglockner is a glaciated white edifice that zooms to 12,457 feet (3,797 m). In the German Alps, the Zugspitze, overlooking Bavaria, is angular, muscular, rough, a big-bellied German wrestler, hard of jaw and often frowning. By contrast, France's much higher Mont Blanc, while also imposing, has graceful lines. From a distance its many ice slopes shimmer and shine innocently in the softest tints. Mont Blanc, at 15,781 feet (4,810 m), is supreme among the

Alps. Lord Byron called it "the Monarch of the Mountains." The poet saw it "in a robe of clouds—with a diadem of snow."

Even Horace Benedict de Saussure, a distinguished Geneva naturalist, was smitten when he saw the monarch for the first time. This was in 1760, and de Saussure confessed to an immediate "aching of desire" for Europe's tallest peak. Why would this wealthy, well-educated nobleman fall in love with a succession of glacial gradients? Why did he aspire to the impossible French summit? According to his contemporaries, de Saussure was a mountain worshiper, as well as a geologist, physicist, and meteorologist. Mont Blanc seemed ideal for this naturalist's atmospheric research. The local people assured de Saussure that the peak was unclimbable, but he refused to believe it. He offered a reward to the first man bold enough to reach the summit. A number of local peasants attempted it but failed. In due time the urge prodded de Saussure himself. But who would brave the perils with him? He couldn't climb alone and he was unable to find allies. Indeed, his fond dream was not to come true until twenty-seven years later—twelve months after Mont Blanc had finally yielded to a Chamonix physician and to a rock hunter.

On August 20, 1787, de Saussure set out in the company of eighteen mountain guides and his valet. Two days later he at last got his wish. He struggled to the top of Mont Blanc, but not without problems. The glare made him half blind, his fingers were numbed by the cold. Despite it all, de Saussure enthusiastically took in the views and then pursued his scientific quests. He returned safely to Geneva with information on air pressure and boiling points at high altitudes.

In due time the Mont Blanc region became a headquarters and proving ground for leading alpinists like Gaston Rébuffat, Maurice Herzog, Lionel Terray, and Walter Bonatti. The French Haute-Savoie Alps and the Dauphine Mountains dazzle visually and acoustically. The names of the peaks and rocks all make music: the Dent du Géant (Giant's Tooth), the Dent Blanche (White Tooth), Aiguille Verte (Green Needle), the Fontaine Ardente (Burning Fountain).

Is there a peak so extraordinary that its form stays with the viewer for a lifetime? One immediately thinks of the world's highest eminences, of Kanchenjunga perhaps, or Makalu, K-2, or Everest itself. But how many people get to see a Himalaya? Or one of the Andean kings?

The famous trio of the Bernese Oberland make a more likely destination. Or the 14,698-foot (4,480-m) Matterhorn, a sharp, solitary, utterly beautiful pyramid. It appears in countless photos as the symbol of the Alps, of Switzerland, and even of Italy. (Half of the Matterhorn is Italian; they call it Monte Cervino.) The roofs of Zermatt are scattered under the peak on the Swiss side, where I once waited three winter days while the Matterhorn hid in clouds. On the fourth day I skied through a storm over the peak's wide ankles. That night the sky cleared. The moon was pure silver. The monolith shone silently, an icy apparition.

The famous peak remains coveted, but it is not unreachable. In fact, each year hundreds of people scramble to the top. Local guides are plentiful. The ascent is considered routine; it takes from six to nine hours.

This was not always the case. Even during the early eighteenth century, local men didn't dare to go up all the way. A few hopefuls tried and were turned back. Some perished. Then in 1860, an English publisher sent young Edward Whymper, a wood engraver and painter, to sketch the Matterhorn for a book. The artist promptly fell under the spell of a mountain "which yet remained virgin," as he later put it. Whymper's ardor and excitement became even greater when he began to explore the peak. He chose the Italian side for his route to the top, trying and failing seven times.

It took until July 14, 1865, for Whymper—and his party of seven—to claim the summit. On the way down, one of the ropes broke. The Matterhorn exacted its price. All but three of Whymper's men plunged four thousand feet to their death.

The same rocks now see climbers with excellent equipment. At lower elevations vacationers use the well-trodden paths, and families enjoy warm meadows with thousands of mountain flowers. Skiers frolic here in winter and spring. Tourists bask on restaurant terraces in the sunshine. Some fine hotels stand within a stone's throw of the churchyard where Whymper's Matterhorn companions lie buried.

2

2

Mountain Diversity

*Preceding pages: Clouds
wreath Huascarán, an extinct
volcano in Peru which is
one of the highest points in
the Andes, the cordillera,
or "little string," running
the length of South America
from Panama to Cape Horn.
Above: Two sluggish glaciers
merge near Monte Rosa,
in the Pennine Alps between
Switzerland and Italy.*

Mountains are the most conspicuous marks on the face of the earth. They rim most continents, diking the seas and marking the lines of weakness in the earth's crust. Some rise in the interior of continents, others in the depths of the seas. From pole to pole and encircling the globe, there are mountains in a diversity of shapes and sizes.

A mountain is defined in relation to the land around it. In otherwise flat country, a rise of only a few hundred feet suffices, at least to the local populace, to bear the label of mountain, though this same mound would not rate even a mention in the shadow of some of the mountain world's giants. Defining a mountain presents a problem even for geologists. Some are satisfied to say that a mountain is any land lifted with considerable abruptness above the adjacent landscape, but others insist that to be deserving of the name a mountain must have a minimum of 2,000 feet (610 m) elevation. Anything less than that is a hill. But with 2,000 feet as the criterion, well over a quarter of the earth's land surface qualifies as high country.

Mountains are much easier to describe than to define. Here we are concerned with the major eminences of land. Rarely do mountains stand alone, though monoliths or monadnocks do occur as single remnants of once greater masses. A group of peaks in the same area, each separated from its companions by a distinct valley, form a massif, a term derived from the French for "massive." A still larger unit in mountain terminology is the mountain range, which refers to a group of peaks that share the same origin. Mountain ranges generally consist of several parallel ridges separated by longitudinal valleys. A group of ranges joined together and arranged in the same direction form a mountain chain, sometimes referred to as a mountain system or cordillera, from the Spanish for "rope" or "belt." Mountain systems cover vast areas.

What are the world's major mountain systems? In which direction do they run, and what are some of their notable peaks?

Starting far north in North America and sweeping southward for more than three thousand miles are the Rocky Mountains, a major cordillera. They are paralleled to the west by several ranges that hug the coast: the Alaska-Canadian Coast Range, the Cascades, the Sierra Nevada, and the Sierra Madre. Among their highest points are 23,320-foot (7,108-m) Mount McKinley in Alaska and 19,850-foot (6,050-m) Mount Logan in Canada. In the United States, top elevations are 14,495-foot (4,418-m) Mount Whitney in the Sierras, 14,162-foot (4,317-m) Mount Shasta in the Cascades, and 14,410-foot (4,392-m) Mount Harvard in the heart of the Rockies. Mexico's Sierra Madre Oriental boasts several towering peaks —18,855-foot (5,747-m) Citlaltepetl and 17,887-foot (5,452-m) Popocatepetl.

From a hundred to as much as four hundred miles wide and four thousand five hundred miles long, the Andes frame the western coast of South America, traversing several nations. Within this giant system are such prominent ranges as the Sierra Nevada de Me-

Antarctica (l) is studded with mountains, some as high as 15,000 ft (4,572 m), whose glaciers extrude huge icebergs into the sea. Top: Rumbalara Hills rise from Simpson Desert of central Australia. Above: Clouds sink below level of Ethiopian escarpment. Northwestern Ethiopia, like Tibet and Andes, is among the highest inhabited regions of the world.

39

rida in Venezuela, the Cordillera Occidental and Cordillera Oriental in Colombia, and the Cordillera Real and Cordillera Central in Bolivia. Elevations? At over 22,000 feet, some of these Andean peaks seem to scrape the sky. About three hundred of their summits exceed the highest point in the United States. Top peaks are 22,834-foot (6,960-m) Aconcagua in Argentina, 22,205-foot (6,768-m) Huascarán in Peru, and 20,577-foot (6,272-m) Chimborazo in Ecuador. The Andes run north and south, an extension of the major mountain system and its ranges in North America.

Across the Atlantic, North Africa's Atlas Mountains angle east-west for some twelve hundred miles. The Atlas, too, is broken into several ranges, including the Middle Atlas, the High Atlas, and the Anti-Atlas. The highest peak is Mount Toubkal in Morocco, its elevation 13,661 feet (4,164 m). Africa has other impressive peaks, particularly in the west-central region of the continent. Most notable are Tanzania's twin-peaked Mount Kilimanjaro at 19,340 feet (5,895 m); Mount Kenya at 17,040 feet (5,194 m); and the mist-shrouded "Mountains of the Moon" of Uganda and Zaire's Ruwenzori Range, including Mount Margherita at 16,798 feet (5,120 m). A total of nine summits in equatorial Africa are more than 16,000 feet in elevation, but they are more or less scattered rather than forming a definite system or cordillera.

Europe's Alps occupy about eighty thousand soaring square miles and run roughly from east to west for about eight hundred miles. More than half a dozen countries share the mighty Alps. They dominate Switzerland. Only the northern portion of the nation might qualify as low country, but fingers of the Alps probe even here. The Alps are composed of a number of ranges, including the Bernese, Pennine, Lepontine, Rhaetian, and Bergamasque Alps, and they are walled on the west by the Jura Mountains. Among the highest of the Alps are 15,781-foot (4,810-m) Mont Blanc in France and the 14,698-foot (4,480-m) Matterhorn, 14,803-foot (4,512-m) Weisshorn, and 14,917-foot (4,547-m) Dom in Switzerland. Monte Rosa towers at 15,209 feet (4,636 m) on the Swiss-Italian border.

The world's highest and longest mountain system, the Himalayas, curve from east to west for almost twice the distance of the Alps. (See pages 46–55.)

By comparison, the Russian Urals are midgets, their summits seldom exceeding a mile above sea level. But the chain is a long one, stretching for sixteen hundred miles from the Arctic Ocean in the north to the Caspian Sea in the south, a barrier between European Russia and the vastness of Siberia. Farther east are the Japanese Alps, a dramatic north-south system composed of about half a dozen ranges with the highest peaks in the Fuji volcanic group. Fujiyama stands 10,456 feet (3,187. m) above sea level; Mount Ontake, 10,444 feet (3,183 m).

Australia's two-thousand-mile Great Dividing Range also runs north-south, its highest point 7,310-foot (2,228-m) Mount

Kosciusko. Still another north-south range, extending for about two hundred miles, is the Southern Alps of New Zealand. Throughout the South Pacific there are numerous islands that consist almost wholly of mountain peaks. High points are 16,503-foot (5,030-m) Cartensz Toppen in New Guinea and 13,455-foot (4,101-m) Mount Kinabalu on Borneo. The loftiest peaks in the Hawaiian Islands (which are themselves mountaintops that jut out above the surface of the sea) are Mauna Kea, 13,796 feet (4,205 m) above sea level, and Mauna Loa, 13,680 feet (4,170 m), both on the island of Hawaii. Like most mountains in the South Pacific, they are volcanic.

Literally scores of mountain ranges help to shape the earth. In the United States there are the comparatively gentle, time-worn Appalachian Mountains, stretching for some fifteen hundred miles along the east coast. Within this giant system are smaller but distinctive ranges: the Blue Ridge Mountains, extending from West Virginia to Georgia; the Adirondacks of New York; the Green Mountains of Vermont; and the White Mountains of New Hampshire. This last range boasts the highest peak in the northeastern United States—6,288-foot (1,917-m) Mount Washington. The highest peak east of the Mississippi is 6,684-foot (2,037-m) Mount Mitchell in North Carolina. Clingman's Dome, on the border of Tennessee and North Carolina, is a close second at 6,642 feet (2,025 m).

Like the Appalachians, England's much shorter Pennines have been ma-tured and rounded by geologic time. The Northwest Highlands and Grampian Mountains of Scotland are more rugged, but even so, their highest peak, Ben Nevis, is only 4,406 feet (1,343 m).

Other well-known mountain ranges are the 270-mile Pyrenees, separating France and Spain; the Apennines in Italy; the Caucasus in the USSR; and the Aleutians, which form stepping stones seaward from Alaska. Many glaciated ranges are scattered over the Arctic and the Antarctic. In the Antarctic, a number of icy crags split the sky, the highest being the 16,860-foot (5,139-m) Vinson Massif.

Mountains form a substantial part of the undersea world, too. The Atlantic Ridge is the world's largest mountain system, more than twice as wide as the Andes and stretching for some ten thousand miles from just off Iceland southward to the tip of Africa. Located almost in the middle of the Atlantic Ocean, most of its peaks are well under the sea, but a few emerge as islands above the surface. The Azores are a group of such peaks. The tallest of them, Pico Island, rises 8,000 feet above sea level; measured from the ocean floor, its elevation is 27,000 feet (8,230 m). Explorers use sophisticated sounding equipment from submarines or the decks of surface research vessels to chart the undersea world, measuring and naming mountains we will never see.

All mountains were not born at the same time in the earth's history. Indeed, mountain origins span a mind-boggling num-

Above: Chimborazo is an inactive volcano and highest point in Ecuadoran Andes, whose furrowed folds are also at right. Right: Mexico's volcanic Popocatepetl. Opposite: Tullujuto in Peruvian Andes.

42

*Pyrenees, running 280 miles
from Bay of Biscay to Mediterranean, have
been a historic barrier between
France and Spain. Streams on Spanish side
(l) generate hydroelectric power.*

ber of years. Which are the world's oldest? Which are the youngest?

Among the oldest are the Russian Urals, dating to at least 400 million years ago. Almost as ancient are the forerunners of the present-day Appalachians in the United States and the Pennines that form England's spine. Their building, or orogeny, continued for a hundred million years or longer before they matured and settled into the shapes we know today.

By comparison the South American Andes are middle-aged, no more than 200 million years old. Geologists say their formation continued until perhaps as recently as 70 million years ago. Crustal convulsions of 60 to 70 million years ago also pushed the present-day Alps into position, and at approximately the same time, fierce uplifts created part of the Rockies. The Himalayas are younger— scientists calculate that their summits may have arisen as recently as 40 million years ago. Probably the youngest of all is the California Coast Range, uplifted less than 25 million years ago, with some upheavals taking place in recent times—about half a million years ago.

But even the most modern methods of radioactive dating can establish only approximate ages, and geologists, continually exploring theories to explain how mountain systems were created, do not always agree with these timetables. They all acknowledge, though, that mountain building can be a complex process that lasts many millions of years. Some systems, such as the Rockies, are second-

time appearances of mighty mountains in the same region, the first having long ago been worn away.

In the past two decades, scientists probing and charting the ocean floor have developed new ideas about mountain building. Geologists are in general agreement now that the earth's crust consists of separate plates that float on the viscous mantle. They drift slowly, actually moving only a few inches a year. When they move apart, molten materials rise from inside the earth to fill the gap and rejoin the edges. But when the plates pull apart, their opposite edges come together or collide with the next adjacent plates.

If the plates have been moving rapidly, which means two or three inches per year, one plate generally rides over the other, the edge of the lower plate sliding into the earth's interior for a hundred miles or more. There it is absorbed. Where the two plates have met, a trench is formed, and the earth's crust is ruptured at this juncture. Volcanoes erupt as heated materials from inside the earth escape through vents. The volcanic islands in the sea originated in such a manner, as did the tremendous undersea trenches and their accompanying deeps.

If the plates have been moving more slowly, they push against each other and buckle, creating a long and ragged ridge of new mountains. The network of undersea mountain ranges that link the various oceans were formed in this way, the materials of the mountains originally on the ocean floor or in the earth's crust.

45

continued on Page 56

The Roof of the World

Perhaps the least-known and most exotic area on earth is the vast homeland of the gigantic mountain systems of Asia. Stretching two thousand miles east and west, from China to Iran, and twelve hundred miles north and south, from Mongolia's Altai to India's Himalayas, it is an awesome geological structure with tier upon tier of great barrier ranges, nearly impenetrable, nearly uninhabited, mostly unexplored, and crenelated with hundreds of the world's highest peaks. Truly, it is "the Roof of the World."

Increasingly, though not yet universally, geographers, geologists, and other scientists believe that these immense wrinkles in the earth's surface are the result of continental drift and collision. Specifically, the Indian subcontinent appears to be advancing northward, slowly but irresistibly, crunching further into the land mass of Asia and buckling the crust along the line of impact. Since the forces of compression are almost unimaginably great, land is displaced, faults and fractures appear, chasms are riven, mountains are heaved up, and the region, already awesome in all its properties and dimensions, is further subjected to the violence of earthquakes.

The elements of this geographical mélange are—like a rumpled suit—complicated to describe. And each, in addition to its own physical inaccessibility, serves as the enclosing rim or boundary to one of the remote spaces of the earth. Thus it is that in the twentieth century only a sparse population of indigenous farmers and herders, a few scientists, and a small but persistent stream of mountain-climbing sportsmen can be said to have experienced the reality of these ranges.

Most familiar, both because they are easily approached and seen, and because they are the home of lofty Everest, the world's highest and most famous peak, are the Himalayas. The word is Sanskrit and means "the Abode of Snow," and indeed the Himalayas are snow-clad throughout their length. They demark the northern edge of Pakistan, India, and the Buddhist kingdoms of Nepal, Sikkim, and Bhutan; beyond them is the

46

Khumbu icefall, en route to Everest.

high plateau of Tibet.

There are Himalayan foothills and lesser ranges building up from the Indian plain, but the heights are two great parallels separated by a wide valley. Here the Indus and Brahmaputra rivers run, one west, the other east, both drawing nourishment from the eternal snows and finding their source in what may have been the original zone of collision between India and Asia.

As mountain systems go, the Himalayas are relatively young, perhaps twenty-five to seventy million years, and still growing. The so-called Great Himalayas—the main backbone—average more than 20,000 feet (6,096 m) and contain thirty peaks rising more than 25,000 feet (7,620 m), among them five of the world's six highest: Everest, Kanchenjunga, Makalu, Dhaulagiri, and Annapurna. Many more peaks still are unknown, unnamed, and unclimbed.

The splendor of the mountains has caused them to be venerated as the seat of the gods and thus as sacrosanct. Peaks are imaginatively named—Thousand Demons, Path to Heaven, Where Only the Horse of the Devil Can Go, and, of course, Goddess Mother of the Earth, which is Everest—and Indian peasants still attribute blights, floods, pestilence, and other natural disasters to the displeasure of mountain divinities. But this awe has contributed—together with the enormous physical obstacles—to a pervasive lack of knowledge about the great ranges.

Despite historic invasions through the passes and the journeys of mercantile travelers such as Marco Polo, the mountains were not mapped with any accuracy until a Spanish missionary to the court of the Mogul emperor Akbar sketched the Himalayas in 1590. Venturesome brothers spreading the True Faith penetrated as far as Lhasa, the Tibetan citadel of Buddhism, in the early eighteenth century, but it was not until scientists and surveyors got to work that the extent of the Himalayas was recognized. Until 1845 South America's Andes were believed

to be the world's highest mountains. Then Dhaulagiri, northwest of Katmandu in Nepal, was found to be higher (26,810 ft/8,172 m) than Ecuador's Chimborazo (20,577 ft/6,272 m), Kanchenjunga (28,168 ft/8,586 m) was found to exceed Dhaulagiri, and Everest (29,028 ft/8,848 m) was found to be supreme.

Everest—Chomolungma, "Goddess Mother," to the Tibetans—was Peak 15 to the British until 1865, when they decided to honor George Everest, surveyor-general and superintendent of the Great Trigonometrical Survey of 1823–47 which established the system of triangulation enabling the peaks to be located and their heights precisely measured. As it

happened, however, Everest did not measure Everest. It was not pegged until 1852. The currently accepted height allows some thirty feet either way for snow at the summit.

As the technical expertise of the world's mountain climbers increased, it was inevitable that they should attempt the world's lordliest tower. Initially, Nepal closed its borders to foreigners, so that all approaches had to be made from Darjeeling, in far northeastern India, through Sikkim, into Tibet, and around in a circular route to the mountain's southwestern face. Eight major expeditions were mounted before the great peak yielded its summit in 1953.

The mountain systems west of the Himalayas and into which they blend can be said to have their center in the Pamirs. This is a geological knot sitting principally in the Tadzhik Republic of the Soviet Union, but also extending into northeastern Afghanistan and southwestern Sinkiang, the westernmost province of the People's Republic of China.

The snow-capped Pamirs have many peaks above 20,000 feet (6,096 m), including Pik Kommunism, which at 24,590 feet (7,495 m) is the highest in the USSR. The nearly treeless region endures long cold winters and not very warm summers. Nomads herding sheep in upland meadows are about the only folks making a living in this inhospitable area.

Annapurna rises over peaceful Nepalese landscape.

Western Systems: Karakorams (l),
Alatau, part of Tien Shan Range in Kirghiz
Soviet Republic (top), and Hindu
Kush in Afghanistan.

The Roof of the World

From the hub of the Pamirs other massive systems radiate: the Hindu Kush, Karakorams, Tien Shan, Kunlun, and Altyn Tagh.

The Hindu Kush, lying mostly in Afghanistan, although penetrating eastward as well into Pakistan and Kashmir, has many high peaks and some of the lowest passes—most notably the Khyber—which give access to the Indian subcontinent. Alexander the Great passed this way on his memorable campaign of conquest in the fourth century B.C. To the ancient world the range was known as the Caucasus Indicus; Alexander's Greeks called it *Parapanisos*—"higher than the eagle's flight." And with their precipitous gorges, bleak, windblown ridges, and trackless glaciers they were indeed formidable. The troops were reduced, say the chronicles, to eating raw mutton flavored with asafetida, a root used as a condiment by those who can stomach its powerful, garlicky smell.

With persistence and the courageous leadership of Iskander, or Secundra (to this day this part of the world is dotted with sites and cities bearing his name or permutations of it), the army pressed on. Eventually it made its way through the 11,600-foot (3,436-m) Khowah Pass to the plains of ancient Bactria, one of whose princesses Alexander took to wife, and on into India, where fever ended the young king's great adventure.

In their turn, the ravaging Mongol hordes of Genghis Khan and Tamerlane cut through the area like a scythe, and after them their sixteenth-century descendant Babur Khan, the founder of the Mogul dynasty that ruled India until another race of invaders, the all-conquering British imperialists, replaced them.

It was in these times of troubles that the mountains earned their contemporary name. Hindu Kush means "Hindu killer," a reference to the Hindu plainsmen who died in the thin air of the heights as they were dragged off to slavery by the marauders.

Today it is no longer the high road to conquest. Its principal peak is Tirich Mir (25,263 ft/7,700 m) from whose summit it is possible to see Pakistan, Kashmir, Afghanistan, the USSR, China, India, and—on a clear day—Tibet. Legend holds that atop the peak there is an enchanted castle guarded by giant frogs.

The Karakorams of Kashmir intersect with the Indian Himalayas, the Soviet Pamirs, and the Afghan Hindu Kush. The word is Turki, meaning "black ground," an apt description of the rocky terrain of the area. The Karakorams are regularly racked by earthquakes, but are rich in minerals (copper, gold, garnets) and fertile for farming. Its upland valleys produce grains, peas, beans, grapes, and apricots.

It is the home of two gigantic peaks: K-2, or Godwin Austen, second only to Everest at 28,250 feet (8,611 m), and Nanga Parbat—"Naked Mountain"—which is a respectable 26,660 feet (8,126 m). Henry H. Godwin Austen was a British topographer and geologist who did pioneering surveys in the Karakorams in the 1850s. The great British mountaineer Eric Shipton likened a climber on the upper part of Everest to "a sick man climbing in a dream." K-2 and Nanga Parbat offer challenges equally fierce. The early British alpinist A. F. Mummery fell to his death on Nanga Parbat in 1895, the first of thirty-one victims before the peak finally was surmounted by a German expedition in 1953, a month after Hillary and Tenzing Norgay climbed Everest. The final assault on Nanga Parbat was made by a single climber, an Austrian who negotiated the great height without oxygen, although in blessedly clear weather. An Italian team achieved K-2 for the first time the following year.

The mountains of Central Asia were perhaps better known five hundred or more years ago, when merchant caravans traveled the exotic trade routes from China, through Samarkand and Tashkent to Europe, and over the high passes into India and Persia. Now they are part of the remoteness of the Soviet Union.

The Tien Shan, or Celestial Mountains,

Pik Kommunism, highest point in Soviet Union, rises in background of Pamir panorama (top). Scale can be judged by view of camel caravan en route to Afghanistan from Kirghizia. Left: Prosaic highway winds through legendary Khyber Pass.

The Roof of the World

run northeast from the Pamirs some fifteen hundred miles to the China-Mongolia border. The highest point is Pobeda Peak (24,406 ft/7,439 m) on the Soviet-Chinese boundary.

The Altai, a geologically complex system, is largely in Kazakhstan, but extends to Mongolia's Gobi Desert and into North China. This is a well-watered region of some three thousand lakes, and rivers fed by the meltwater from two hundred thirty square miles of glaciers. The lower slopes are densely forested and in the eastern part of the range are deposits of silver, first mined by Russians in the seventeenth century, as well as gold, mercury, iron, lead, zinc, copper.

The Kunlun, another offshoot of the Pamirs, extends some one thousand miles east along the Tibet-Sinkiang border, between the Himalayas and the Tien Shan. Streams rising on the north slope of this range are swallowed in the desert sands of Sinkiang.

The Altyn Tagh, also north of the Himalayas and parallel to them, have been the subject of photographic fly-overs by National Aviation and Space Agency satellites which reveal geological faults and shifts too massive to be judged from the ground. They seem to support the tectonic-plate theory of continental collision and incidental mountain formation.

For all their inaccessibility—perhaps because of it—these mountains of Asia abound in wildlife. There are bear and yak; India's bison, the gaur; musk and barking deer; markhor, bharal, tahr, and other mountain sheep and goats; China's raccoon-related panda; stone marten; marmots. There are vultures, mallard ducks, and butterflies up to 10,000 feet. The Karakorams have forty-five varieties of snakes. There is rain forest, lush and dank, in the foothills of the Himalayas. There are mountain wildflowers in the upland meadows.

Eventually, however, all thins out in the rarefied atmosphere and eternal snows of the summits. Except for the howls of the wind and the whoosh of the avalanche, all is still on the Roof of the World.

54

On approaches to Everest. Ama Dablam (r) is a mere 22,350 ft (6,812 m).

As a result of receding seas and later movements of the earth's crust, the rocks of some former undersea mountain ridges were lifted high above sea level. This explains why the fossils of sea animals have been found high in the Alps, 'for example, a puzzle to early-day scientists.

The movement of plates in the earth's crust as an explanation of mountain building does not contradict older theories. Rather, it explains more logically the major mountain systems. Subsequent forces have also been in operation to give the mountains their distinctive shapes and character over the millions of years. Remember that geologic time is quite different from the measure of human history. Rises of only a few inches a year can create mountains thousands of feet high in the span of millions of years, and it takes little longer than that for erosive forces to cut them down again.

Most mountains are gigantic folds in the earth's crust. According to the most widely accepted explanation, the formation of such mountains begins when a huge sea-bottom trough, or geosyncline, fills with sediments over millions of years. Sometimes the sediments may be 30,000 feet or more deep, and over years of compression of layer upon layer, they become hardened into sedimentary rocks. The weight of the rocks and sediments contributes to some degree to the sinking of the trough, but primarily it comes about as a result of convection currents in the earth's plastic mantle. Some of the sedimentary rocks are metamorphosed into still harder rocks as a result of the heat and pressure. As the convection currents complete their revolution, the materials of the geosyncline are folded upward as mountains. Both the Appalachians and the Urals show their origin as sediments of shallow sea floors. At one time the Appalachians were as high as the present-day Alps, but over the years erosive forces have strewn them as sediments over the Atlantic coastal plain.

Other movements in the earth's crust also contribute to the formation and complexity of mountains. The folds, for example, may become multiple, one wrinkle added on top of another. Fractures or faults may occur, so that the various layers of rocks are not aligned as they were when originally laid down. Some of the faults are abrupt movements in the earth's crust, causing earthquakes and the sheer rises of blocks of mountains. California's Sierra Nevada is an example of mountains that were formed by the faulting of a folded mountain range. Their western slope is gradual, but the eastern slope is steep, averaging more than 10,000 feet of rise along the fault line. The Black Hills of South Dakota were formed when a great mass of granite was lifted above the surface as a dome, now eroded to core fragments. New Zealand's Southern Alps also were created in this manner. In some mountains the shifts are almost vertical; in others they are to the side, causing a tilt in the slopes.

Volcanic mountains are those built up around vents through which lava boils or explodes through the earth's crust. Vulcanism is, in fact, the most rapid way that mountains can be built. The speed record belongs to Paracutin, a modest Mexican volcano that popped up in a cornfield in February, 1943, and grew to a height of more than 1,000 feet in less than two years. Cone-shaped volcanoes grow much more rapidly than those that are spread broadly as shields. Several thousand active, dormant, and dead volcanoes make up a significant segment of the mountain world.

One of the most famous active volcanoes is Mount Etna on Sicily. Stromboli, also on Sicily, has been in some state of activity throughout recorded history. Its fiery cone was the "lighthouse of the Mediterranean" that guided early sailors. The Azores, the Canaries, and Madeira—all were produced by volcanic upheavals. Many of the islands off Greece are marked with great cinder heaps of extinct volcanoes. The British Isles and the Scottish Highlands still show traces of lava, and in the Antarctic, giant Mount Erebus is an active volcano standing more than 13,000 feet above sea level.

Japan's famous Fujiyama resulted from the building up of successive lava flows, cinders, and ash to the familiar present-day cone capped with ice and snow. Some of the Hawaiian volcanoes are shield-shaped domes with gentle slopes. Others, like Mauna Loa, are monolithic. More than sixty miles in diameter, Mauna Loa's peak is 13,680 feet above sea level. But there are an additional 18,000 feet of Mauna Loa below the surface of the sea, making its total rise (9,656 m) greater than any other mountain in the world. Oregon's 11,235-foot (3,424-m) Mount Hood emerged from lava ejections through a deep, half-mile-wide crater, and lava also created Africa's Mount Kilimanjaro.

Dormant volcanoes are those that have erupted in geologically recent periods but are now basically quiet, only occasionally spewing out lava or sending up noxious clouds. But more than five hundred volcanoes in the world are still active and may go off at any time, exploding skyward as the hot magma from the earth's interior is ejected as molten lava, ash, cinders, and various gases. Red-hot when it pours from the vent, the lava changes slowly to dark red and then to gray or black as it cools. While still very hot, it has the fluid consistency of hot tar. It oozes slowly, like thick cement, as it cools.

In their studies of volcanoes, scientists frequently turn to Iceland, lying in the Atlantic between Greenland and Norway. At first sight, the thousands of craters forming Iceland's landscape remind visitors of pictures taken on the moon. Even the environs of Reykjavik, the capital, are one black bed of lava, and hot springs are tapped to supply the city's heat. Between the Ice Age and present times, at least a hundred and fifty volcanoes have blasted away on this island. New peaks still pop out of the sea, hissing and smoking as the volcanic activity under the glaciers unleashes sudden flows. In countless spots on the island, steam squeezes through crustal holes and fills the horizon with white clouds. Young volcanic activity produces cascades of red-hot liquid basalt, lighting Iceland's sky with orange and pink—a night-

time extravaganza that could not be duplicated by the Las Vegas neon jungle.

But wherever they exist and no matter how they were formed, as soon as mountains poke skyward, erosive forces—water, wind, and ice—begin whittling them down. The leveling processes are slow but relentless. Erosion gives mountains their distinctive shapes; their colors are determined by the rocks of which they are made.

The "horn" of the Matterhorn in the Alps, for example, was gouged out by glacial action over many centuries. Nothing remains of the original rounded peak but this sharp, rocky core. Many of the Alpine peaks have "horns" of this type. The most powerful of the ice forces came when the great glaciers of the Ice Age swept over the Northern Hemisphere, the first of the four onslaughts beginning about two million years ago and the last ending about ten thousand years ago. The first changes were climatic. The air grew frigid, temperatures averaging some 15 degrees lower than now. Hail gunned the highlands, and then the freezing-cold rain turned into blizzards that heaped the landscape with white.

Snowfields were compacted by their own weight into a granular moving mass called a névé. Motion generates pressure which contributes to the eventual transformation of the mass into ice. Friction slows movement, so that glaciers move faster in the center than on the sides, faster on top than on the bottom. Pressure also causes the irregularly shaped ice crystals to melt and to re-form when pressure is relieved. Hence the continually changing shape of glacier mass.

Over thousands of years, some glaciers grew to as much as two miles in thickness. They slid southward from Siberia, Canada, and Scandinavia until they covered at least a third of the earth's surface. Then came a warm period, followed again by cold and glaciation. Four times, in fact, the glaciers rode down over the continents, each period lasting from 50,000 to 100,000 years.

Each time, the glaciers did their work of grinding and gouging, scraping and polishing. Pushed ahead of the slow-moving sheets of ice were soils, loose rocks, and even giant boulders, helping to abrade the land over which they rode. The great sheets of ice slid over the mountains of eastern North America —the Green, the White, and the Adirondacks— and over the mountains of the British Isles. They trimmed their tops and gentled them, leaving wherever they passed a much more subdued and rounded landscape. At their southern extremities, where they had lost some of their wallop, the glaciers left jagged mountain peaks, cut into but not demolished. Ice Age glaciers transformed the entire landscape of most of the Northern Hemisphere.

Scientists remind us that today we are probably living in an interglacial stage. The great ice masses that once covered vast portions of the continents have now retreated and are confined to the polar regions. They are poised there, ready to descend again when conditions are right. And there are still glaciers

*Massive split rock of Half Dome,
in California's Yosemite National Park,
is part of the Sierra Nevada.
Smooth, bald surfaces like these are
difficult, if not impossible, to climb.*

aplenty in the mountain world—about two thousand in all. They are found most abundantly in mountains in cold regions, of course, but there are glaciers, too, in the high mountains of the tropics—the Himalayas, the Andes, and the peaks of equatorial Africa. Many mountaintops of the Alps, the Caucasus, the Sierras, the Rockies, and the Cascades are capped with ice, too. Unlike the continental sheets, mountain glaciers become sculptors of single edifices. The spectacular granite fortresses of Yosemite—El Capitan, for example —are products of glacial sculpting, as are many other of the world's mountains.

I have flown over many glaciated mountain regions and have climbed a number of large glaciated peaks where the ice is still at work, plowing and furrowing as the mass slips slowly down the slopes. These snowy, icy pinnacles are strangely silent worlds. Their surfaces can glare like a thousand sun-reflecting mirrors. Some seem to be all icy angles, the long ice fields knifed by short, darker lines of fissures. A glacier may be hollowed with caves, shafts, and hidden but noisy streams, and there are overhangs and cornices, marked by enormous fingerlike icicles. Some may appear to be soft and friendly, but the white snow can hide crevasses hundreds of feet deep. Mountain glaciers leave an indelible impression.

Mount Rainier, dwarfing its rivals in the Pacific Northwest, offers isolation in its glaciers, despite the mountain's closeness to Seattle. Most tourists do not go higher than

5,400 feet, where, at Paradise Valley, telescopes permit them to inspect the mountain's glaciers in comfort and safety. Higher up—at 10,000 feet—is Camp Muir, requiring half a day of uphill plodding. Glacier guides and their clients use this camp as their base for still higher trips to visit one or several of Mount Rainier's more than two dozen glaciers, each of which is named. Like other giants of the Cascades, Mount Rainier began as a volcano, its last eruption nearly two thousand years ago, but now the glaciers are reshaping the mountain. In sheer power these moving masses of ice are the strongest of the erosive forces at work on the mountains.

Mountain glaciers consist of snow that has been compressed into ice a hundred feet or more in thickness. As it tongues its way down the slope, pushing debris ahead of it, the glacier hews and planes a valley into the slope. Where it pulls away from the mountainside, it tears huge segments of rocks. In many places, as in the Bernese Oberland in Switzerland and the Tetons of the American West, the glaciers carve out an amphitheaterlike valley, or cirque. The walls rise abruptly as cliffs, and typically there is a pond or small lake in the basin of the valley. Glacial valleys are broad and U-shaped, easily distinguished from the sharply V-shaped valleys cut by streams. The smooth, steep sides of old cirques become furrowed by erosion.

Running water also shapes mountains; in fact, its total effect in the mountain world has been much greater than that of

Many of the world's mountains are volcanic piles in various states of quiescence or activity. Spectacular violence (l) is eruption in progress on island off Iceland. Top: Sicily's Etna, momentarily inert. Above: Lenticular cloud hovers above crest of Mikeno, a volcano in Albert National Park, in Zaire.

63

*Mesas of Arizona's Monument
Valley are remnants of a plateau eroded
by weather. Table tops were the
original ground level. Towers
are a test for any climber.*

glaciation. Erosion begins when a single drop of rain bombards the surface, bouncing tiny particles into movement. In heavy rains, billions of drops fall on the slopes, first moving downward as a thin sheet of water, then collecting to form rivulets, and finally rampaging down the mountain as a brook. The faster the water runs, the more cutting power it has, and the greater the load of sediment and debris it can carry. All these particles, from the tiniest fragments to large boulders tumbled by the swift water, act as abrasives, too, slicing into the mountain slopes. In waterfalls and cascades, the water may be traveling sixty miles an hour or faster, and when it hits the earth, it digs in deeply. This increases the height of the waterfall, but at the same time the brink of the waterfall is cut back year by year, making the gorge longer as well as deeper.

Running waters leave variously sculptured slopes behind them. Some of the rock formations wash away more quickly than others, but the erosion often shows more clearly the layered markings of a mountain, the formations in some looking pleated and in others strongly wrinkled and disordered. In western North America, the flat-topped mesas and the similar but smaller buttes are prime examples of remnants of erosion, mainly by water. Some, such as Devil's Tower in Wyoming, stand as volcanic skeletons—columnar spires with only lava ribs remaining. Colors, too, stand out spectacularly. The pillars in Colorado's Garden of the Gods and in the Flatirons owe their bright color to red sandstone, which

also gives many peaks of the West their delightful hues of red, pink, and purple.

Water works on mountains not only mechanically but also chemically. Combined with elements of the atmosphere and with the components of the rocks themselves, the water acts both as a solvent and, in some cases, as an acid, eating away and decaying the rocks. Limestone is particularly subject to chemical weathering, dissolving and wearing down much more quickly than the more resistant and harder metamorphosed or igneous rocks. Classic examples are the craggy, jagged limestone towers of the Dolomites in the Italian Alps. The white slopes of Carrara are of more resistant white marble, the stone sought by Michelangelo and other great sculptors and exposed as a basic raw material by the erosive forces of nature.

In arid and semiarid regions, wind is an important agent in shaping mountains. Many of the sandstone mesas and buttes of the West were tooled into their present shapes by the grinding action of sand particles and rock fragments driven against the rock masses by the wind. Even the sea is a powerful erosive force where the mountains are close to the coast. In the Maritime Alps, shared by France and Italy, the sea has carved high cliffs and bluffs that now overlook popular resort beaches.

Rarely is a mountain acted upon by only a single erosional process. It is shaped by the interaction of many forces over long periods of time. Rocks are heated in day-

68

time, then fracture at night when temperatures
drop suddenly. They are split apart by the alter-
nate freezing and thawing of water seeping
through their fissures, and by the roots of trees
or even smaller plants. Burrowing animals
open up new avenues into which water percolates and flows to weather the rocks and soil
both mechanically and chemically. Wind, water, and ice may wear away only one layer of
rocks in a formation, but in time this single
action may undercut a tremendous section of a
mountainside and cause it to break off or
slump. Each erosive activity opens the mountain to still other kinds of erosion, and always
the force of gravity pulls. Mountains everywhere are constantly being scarred, seamed,
and gnawed at.

However they were formed
and then molded, the mountains we see today
are by no means final products. We see them in
only one stage of their evolution. They may be
young, mature, or old, their diversity as varied
as the earth from which they were pushed and
then shaped. Year by year the mountain world
changes, old peaks and even entire ranges disappearing while new ones take their place on the
mobile face of the earth.

3

3

Mountain Moods

*Gradations of light,
shifts in weather, or the
progress of the seasons can
work dramatic changes
in a mountain's appearance.
Preceding pages: Last light on
the Himalayas. Above:
Geometry of Death Valley.*

72

Mountain moods fluctuate with the hour, the season, and the weather. The time of day governs the light by which great peaks and ranges are seen. Dawn, noon, twilight—each has a subtle effect on the subdued colors of stone, tinting them rose red, sun yellow, or prism violet by turns. The transit of the sun through the heavens is marked by advancing and retreating shadows, vast blacknesses briefly obliterating slopes and facets or dulling the gleam of a valley.

The boundaries of the seasons are determined by temperature. Summer warmth enhances the beneficent greens of mountainside forests. Cool autumn is red and gold. Winter is black and white. Transitional spring reasserts the color patterns of life and growth, and the snow line recedes toward its last bastion on the summits.

Weather seems more immediate in the mountains. The higher one goes, the purer the sun's rays, the closer the clouds, the more turbulent the air. Climatologists reckon a drop in temperature for every few hundred feet of elevation. Each thousand feet up the Rockies lowers the air temperature to that at ground level two hundred miles farther north. By lying athwart the path of weather and intercepting rain clouds, mountain ranges can determine the climate of vast areas of land, visiting moisture on one slope while condemning the opposite one to heat and aridity.

To this long-time wanderer, mountains always are lessons in meteorology. Early Sunday at the foot of Ben Nevis, the pride of the Scottish Highlands: a summer sun is as bright as the breakfast eggs. The trail winds and climbs through deep green ferns, past knee-high wild grasses. A few hundred feet higher appears a sudden rivulet. I study Ben Nevis's upper region. Dark clouds loom.

Hike to the 1,000-foot level (c. 330 m). Below, the lochs glisten. In the valleys are well-demarcated fields. The precious sun is soon diluted, turning to the palest yellow. The watery trail makes me wonder: is it raining on the summit? Step by step up the now-bare bulky mountain to about 2,000 feet (c. 650 m). The finest imaginable wetness runs down my temples, cheeks, hands. I slip into a poncho; the water courses down its waxen folds. At about 2,500 feet the wind suddenly whistles down a rocky crest. The gust seizes my Scots garment. I am a mariner in the stormy North Sea, alone on deck, facing the gray sky in an oilcloth slicker. Then the wind subsides and goes elsewhere. On the British Isles' highest peak it is calm once more. I have Ben Nevis to myself.

It turns colder. I am not tempted to stop and rest. The valley has disappeared. Slow progress up staircases of squishing bogs. At 3,000 feet (c. 1000 m) the rivulet has turned into a small river, complicating my navigation of the trail. Fort William, the town at the mountain's base, no longer exists. The roofs are hidden under bales of white cotton.

The wavy sea of clouds below is a familiar sight to people who spend time in the high country. The white ocean covers and

73

*Preceding pages: The splendor
and imperturbability of mountains
are conveyed in panorama of Dolomites
from Cortina. New Hampshire's Mount
Washington (r) glows under cloud cap.*

hides the cities of the plain. It is a curious sensation. Alighting, for instance, from a passenger train that has ascended the mountain, one may walk through thick wads of cloud, although the peak and the white-tipped triangles of other pinnacles piercing the billowing sea are stark against a sapphire-blue sky.

Ben Nevis's rain stops and sunbeams relight the world. I roll up the poncho and put on a sweater for the final stretch. The forces of erosion have done their job well on these ancient Scottish Highlands. The humps are worn smooth. High up, all is talus and scree. The trail coils uphill. At about 3,500 feet the sun retreats again into the brooding heavens. Now I'm walking through veillike clouds. Visibility has been cut to two or three yards. Suddenly I hear steps coming down. Another human being on Nevis? A hiker draws into sight. It is a girl. Wet forehead, wet cheeks, her parka wet. "Not a baaad day," she says in Scottish accent pure. "Not baaad," I echo. The hammering sound of her boots stays with me for a moment, then fades, then ceases.

I have reached roughly 4,000 feet (1,219 m) above sea level. Ben Nevis's summit cairns draw into view. Windy up here. The air currents drill into my neck. But the sky is clear and I am grateful for the unexpected view of Scotland's glens, slopes and boulders, ridges, and waterfalls. I discover a shelter of sorts on the summit. I sit with my back to the crumbling walls of a one-time observatory. Tasty lunch. Well-earned, too. Return to Fort William in blissful sunshine.

The caprices of mountain weather catch some flatlanders by surprise. On occasion an unseasonable warmth greets backpackers bearing goose-down parkas and sleeping bags. In the Rockies an arid chinook wind may blow, melting cornices. In Austria the warm, dry foehn sweeping down the mountains sets the natives' nerves on edge. In New England, 6,288-foot (1,917-m) Mount Washington can be on its worst behavior at the height of the tourist season. Sudden winds arrive, as one hiker put it, "with the speed of gunshots." Washington's gales are notorious. (The record: 231 mph.) Moreover, the top is often immersed in soupy fog. The Scots of Fort William find it easy to joke about Highland weather: "Och, in the next months the thermometer will stay at eighty degrees—forty in the morning and forty in the afternoon!" And of the inhabitants of the moisture-laden high French Alps their more fortunate compatriots of the Côte d'Azur remark: "Look at those poor Savoyards! Why do they have stiff necks? From craning them— *bien sûr*—to see the sun!"

One evening, after having trudged up an Austrian Alp for seven or eight hours, a girl and I chanced into a late fall storm. The sky wept in torrents. Our hiking clothes were no match for this *Unwetter*—this storm. Should we flee to a lower elevation? No, we would stick to our original plans. We would go on up to a primitive shelter known as the Herrmann's *hütte*. It was another soggy sixty minutes away.

In due time its metal roof ap-

Storms lend a terrible
aspect to Muldrow Glacier on
Mount McKinley (below)
and to the Tetons (r)
oppressed by cloud rack
and lowering skies.

peared and we could see the cables that braced the structure. The whole sky was threatening to come down on the roof. No one was in sight at the hut. The door was locked—but my companion had brought the key all the way from the Alpine Club headquarters at Klagenfurt.

The floor was covered with straw. Mattresses were scattered about for sleeping. The wind creaked in the rafters, the cables sang from the strumming of the storm as we put on dry clothes and sweaters. We started a warming blaze in the fireplace. I still remember how we held on to each other, gratefully, while it rained and rained.

Blonde curls drying, the girl then began solemn preparations for a dinner in harmony with our simple surroundings: a tiny piece of country bacon for each of us, two hard rolls, and a liter of hot split-pea soup. We were snug against the raging of the storm outside.

John Muir, finding his day "enlivened with one of the most bracing windstorms," immediately headed into the woods to experience the blow firsthand. "The air," he wrote, "was mottled with pine tassels and bright green plumes that went flashing past in the sunlight like birds pursued. . . . I heard trees falling for hours at the rate of one every two or three minutes; some uprooted . . . others broken straight across. The force of the gale was such that the most steadfast monarch of them all rocked down to its roots with a motion plainly perceptible when one leaned against it. Nature was holding high festival."

The higher one ventures, the more wind one encounters. Winds make temperatures drop and create a "chill factor" that increases the intensity of the cold. At zero degrees Fahrenheit (−17.8 C) on a mountain a twenty-mile-per-hour wind drives the mercury down to −40 F (−40 C).

In the Alps many mountaineers judge the wind according to a scale established in 1800. Like the Beaufort wind scale used at sea, numbers indicate wind strength in terms of observable local phenomena.

0 – No wind.	Chimney smoke goes straight up.
1 – Light breeze.	Smoke blows away.
2 – Light wind.	Wind can be felt on one's face.
3 – Gentle wind.	Tree leaves are in motion.
4 – Moderate wind.	Small branches move.
5 – Animated wind.	Young trees bend.
6 – Stormy wind.	Large branches begin to shake.
7 – Harder wind.	Entire trees bend.
8 – Gale.	Tiles blown off roof.
9 – Powerful storm.	Trees uprooted.
10 – Violent storm.	Serious damage.

Yet storms have the power to cleanse. The adverse weather is swept out of the dome of heaven. The mountain crests shine anew. Or the sun may concentrate like a mighty searchlight on one peak, ignoring all the others.

A climber may stand in sunshine and see clouds engulfing nearby summits, or slanting sheets of gray rain yonder, while his own bailiwick stays dry. Thunderclouds sometimes rumble and growl directly overhead, change their minds, restrain themselves, and take their tears elsewhere. "Only fools and newcomers," goes one Western saying, "forecast mountain weather."

Mountain summers are often short, a pause of a few weeks between the lingering spring snows and the new flakes of autumn. Deep down in the valley shadowlands it gets dark early, anyway. By September the quaking aspens transform themselves into shining beacons, each round leaf pure gold, and any day now a sharp wind may deliver a swarm of snow crystals, for the mountain world does not read the calendar or keep a timetable. Snow may fall while the trees still wear their leaves.

High mountains turn wintry with astonishing swiftness. There may be hardly any warning. Perhaps not even a storm. Just a first snowflake, then another, and soon the birds cease their song and the hillsides disappear behind the white curtain. Denizens of the high country learn to expect the disappearance of their horizon and the early onset of chilling cold. Whether in the Sawtooths of Idaho or the Austrian Tyrol or France's Haute Savoie, defenses must be built against winter. The Swiss farmer of the upland meadows weights down his roof with boulders. He lays in cords of neatly cut wood; his wife has a full larder.

There are gradations of the severity of winter. The U.S. National Weather Service distinguishes carefully among them. Snow flurries are intermittent falls that may reduce visibility but leave only light accumulations. Snow squalls, also brief, are more intense, with gusty surface winds. Freezing drizzle brings a coating of ice. Heavy snow means four to six inches in the next twelve to twenty-four hours. Blizzard means wind speeds of at least 35 mph, considerable falling and/or blowing snow, and temperatures of 20 degrees F (−6.7 C) or less over an extended period. Severe blizzards bring dense snow, 45-mph winds, and 10-degree temperatures (−12.2 C) or less.

Highway crews, utility men, railroaders encounter the full range of winter weather. Hunters regularly get lost in winter storms. Motorists are enveloped in whiteouts and may be stranded, unable to move, for hours. Friedrich Nietzsche, not your ordinary, run-of-the-mill mortal, appears to have welcomed storms. From his Alpine retreat the philosopher wrote a friend, "The storm broke with a mighty clash. I felt inexpressibly well and full of zest!"

In the Tetons December and January may unload up to one hundred inches of snow. On Oregon's Mount Hood a "silver thaw" can glaze the world with a half-inch coat of ice. Crystalline trees bow under the weight. Rocks glint like glass. Roads, houses, steps, benches, balconies, the snowplow, the Volkswagen with the ski rack, the towers of the lift —all are slick and treacherous with ice.

For all the dangers and disrup-

81

Great brow of El Capitan
is mantled in cloud
(below), while crumbling
Sierras (opposite), as seen
from vantage point of
Mount Whitney, sprawl like
disintegrating dinosaur bones.

tions they may bring, however, the snows of winter look soothing and peaceful on a mountainside. Curves and hollows shine in moonlight and sparkle in morning sun. The meadows sleep. And with each fresh fall the traces of man are erased. People who grow up among such snowscapes find it wrenching to leave them.

Yet the mountains can be generous, even opulent. They are the birthplace of rivers, and the runoff of their melting blankets of snow fills the reservoirs of cities hundreds of miles away. The fat Alpine meadows of Switzerland—and elsewhere—nourish chocolate-brown cows, the fount of mountain milk, butter, and cheese. The mountain environment supports abundant wildlife, as well as domesticated herds of grazers and browsers—from the yaks of the Himalayas and the llamas of the Andes to the Aberdeen Angus cattle of Scotland and the goats and sheep of the Caucasus.

Mountain spas have been visited by the sick and ailing since the Middle Ages. Whether to drink the mountain waters, to breathe the mountain air, or to view the serenity of a mountain vista, the pilgrims came. Perhaps the therapy was—and is—principally psychological, a balm, a comfort and an encouragement to the old and ill, a tonic to the still robust. Boccaccio's nobles fled to the hills to escape the pestilence in Florence. Mann's consumptives sought relief—if not a cure—on a magic mountain.

Of all of the mountain benisons, however, perhaps none is the merry cheerer of the heart so much as wine. Chilean vintners credit the Andes for fine wines. The mountain backdrop and the warm breezes are apparently kind to Chile's vineyards. The Alps' steep Rhône valley encourages growth and the bottling of excellent wines in a lovely mountain setting. The vines prosper above Lac Léman and Lac Neuchâtel, and in innumerable Italian *colline*. The mountains of Corsica and the slopes of Oporto and Malaga all make for good grape harvests. Madeira's vineyards angle down to the sea as do those of the French Riviera. North of San Francisco the long Sonoma hillsides get drenched in spring. The vines turn their faces toward the California sun. The grapes ripen. Mountain country, wine country. The Salinas valley, the Napa valley, the Santa Clara valley tell their own story, one of more smiles than sulks.

One of bright sweet air and good moods.

4

Climbing

Secure belaying is first rule of safe and successful climbing. Preceding pages: Anchorman (r) in ancient Scottish Highlands is himself belayed by taut line. Above: Risk of leap across Mount Rainier crevasse is minimized by support from each side.

88

Summer dawn. Forty degrees north and 110 degrees west. A sea of rock in an ocean of mountain, solid against the sky. The last stars are extinguished and pale air hovers over the horizon. In the foreground is a still-dark granite wall. It strains uphill for nearly one thousand feet with a few vertical corrugations. The blocks and slabs make a geometrical pattern. Some of the rock is metal-slick. From a narrow ledge a thin red climbing rope snakes down, following a long crack in the granite.

Is anyone tied to the rope? One's eyes need time to adjust. Yes, two minute human figures, separated by about a hundred feet of stone. Anyone moving? Doesn't look like it. Two tiny figures glued to the faraway rock.

A closer view reveals some motion. One man is inching upward, ever so slowly and cautiously. On the upper ledge his companion—a bearded Greek god—has chained himself to the rock. His powerful arms are now busy with the rope, pulling it up, gradually gathering the slack as the second man climbs. The distance between them narrows foot by foot. But there are long pauses. It will take several hours to ascend less than 80 feet. The two climbers are friends, but the bearded man always leads. More experience.

At about 10:00 A.M. the wall receives the brunt of the western sun. The heat begins. It increases and radiates. The men take canteens out of their day packs and drink. The wall absorbs the sun and throws it back. By noon their shirts show dark ovals of sweat. The rock becomes hot as a griddle. Each handhold causes pain. Gloves? Out of the question. The climbers need to feel their way up, need to reach into tight crevices and cracks, need to test a knob to gauge the strength of a hold. They must have direct contact with the overheated mountain. No gloves, then. The climbers could rub chalk into their sweaty palms. This puts a stop to the perspiration and assures a better hold. But chalk leaves unsightly traces on the rock, and these are purists who wish to leave the mountain as they found it. So they just wipe their wet hands against their pants.

By afternoon they've done two more pitches, roughly another 250 feet. A few tiers make a difference. They now can see more country. A soft mixture of scents—the spruce forests, old conifer needles, meadows awash in summer flowers—reaches them. The climbers breathe deeply. Peace at the lower elevations. Miles away the foothills shimmer. Milky smog covers the distant plains. The two men continue their uphill trip.

What would a spectator see? Not a very dramatic performance. Just a ponderous ascent. Long pauses in the heat. A wall demanding patience and a maximum of forethought. The angle is a steep 85 degrees. To a climber looking down, the wall leans in the manner of an office building. The occasional ledges are no wider than window sills. Yet each section of the journey fills the climbers with satisfaction. They did not come with the intention of actually reaching the top. In this case the ascent itself—not the summit—happens to

89

be the payoff. This is not a virgin wall or a famous mountain. The challenge is a difficult grade with minimal equipment. The total uphill distance does not matter.

The final pitch is about two-thirds up. From here a shelf no wider than a boot sole permits a traverse toward the east face. With the help of some easily removable copper pieces ("nuts") and some "biners"—cara-biners, snap-rings attached to anchors driven into rock cracks—the red rope can be strung all the way across. The precipice would be harrowing and dizzying to a nonclimber or a tyro. But these cragsmen have several years of experience and are used to exposure.

It takes until four in the afternoon to get to the other side. Black thunderheads appear out of nowhere. The climbers wisely prepare for immediate descent. The granite rock drops straight down for 20 feet, then slopes away at about a 40-degree angle. Plenty of ridges and cracks. The men pick a solid slab for a rappel anchor. Boot soles to the rock, backs to the valley, they go down rapidly by means of the rope. The maneuver looks spectacular. The two men descend with the ease of dancers.

They return to the bottom with stinging hands, sunburned faces, and parched throats. Their arms and elbows are scratched and gashed from the rock. But they feel on top of the world, psychologically and physically.

Motivations? Men and women climb to defeat a difficult wall, to achieve total body control, to overcome their fears, or simply for the aesthetics of the experience. Mountaineering can be an exercise in dexterity, an athletic feat, a joyful interplay of motion, rhythm, and balance.

The early British alpinists were eloquent enough about the virtues and joys of climbing. "A noble sport!" wrote Sir Leslie Stephen, athlete and aesthete, author, critic, editor of the *Dictionary of National Biography*, and father of Virginia Woolf. And Edward Whymper: "An endless series of pictures, magnificent in form, effect and color." To this English artist and author, mountaineering was "the music of distant herds, the solemn church bells." Then A. F. Mummery, who climbed in the Caucasus: "The troubles and cares of life are left far below, in the reeking valleys." And, later, George Mallory, lost on an early effort to surmount Everest: "Something sublime is the essence of mountaineering."

Mountaineering—the climbing of mountains for sport, pleasure, and physical well-being—was a nineteenth-century discovery embraced most wholeheartedly by the resolute, outdoorsy British. Like most sports, it evolved when people had money and leisure to pursue it. And the world-wide triumph of British commerce in Victoria's reign released regiments of well-born or well-fixed gentlemen to essay the heights of Europe (as well as to refine golf and tennis into something approximating their present form).

The first important climb for its own sake was an ascent of Mont Blanc in 1786. It was repeated the following year by

Horace Benedict de Saussure, a remarkable Swiss scientist who devoted years to the study of Europe's high-mountain geology, botany, and meteorology. Thereafter the enterprise became general. The Jungfrau, the Finsteraarhorn, and many other peaks were topped, although equipment and techniques were too rudimentary to master the Matterhorn or the Eiger. Parties of ladies in ankle-length dresses, however, were encouraged to ascend glaciers with the help of gentlemen, servants, and a series of ladders.

The Alpine people, who had climbed no more than necessary—out of superstitious fear, or because they had a hard, nonrecreational living to make in the heights—did not take long to realize that there was a source of income in these enthusiasts clamoring to be shown the routes upward. They promptly became guides and, with practice, mountaineers.

Modern mountaineering is considered to have begun around mid-century. Colorado's Wetterhorn was climbed in 1854, and the Matterhorn, by Whymper, in 1865. The Alpine Club, London, was established in this period, and the search for climbing challenges soon spread to other areas. Britons discovered the British Isles: the Lake District, Wales, the Scottish Highlands. Although these mountains were mostly crumpled and ancient hills, without a soaring peak among them, climbers learned that height is not always a measure of difficulty, that cliffs of less than a hundred feet can tax the skills of the most expert.

Other mountaineers ventured into Norway, and the redoubtable Mummery invaded the Caucasus. One by one the peaks were ascended: Wyoming's Grand Teton in 1872, Chimborazo in the Ecuadoran Andes (by Whymper) in 1880, Kilimanjaro in 1889, Aconcagua in 1897, Mount Kenya in 1899, Mount McKinley in 1913. By the nineties, too, there were the first assaults on the giants of the Karakorams and the Himalayas.

It was in the twentieth century, however, that the technical, medical, meteorological, and logistical factors involved in these prodigious climbs were increasingly better understood and applied in a series of expeditions to the great peaks at the roof of the world.

With every mountain, but most particularly with Everest because it is the world's highest and among the more inaccessible, there is always the problem of establishing a route to the top. The approach to Everest from India and Nepal made certain choices inevitable, but for the early expeditions there was guesswork as well. They did not have a precise knowledge of the mountain's structure. Their perspectives on its higher reaches, because of foreshortening in looking up a five-mile height from below, were false and misleading. The summit, more often than not, was obscured by precipitous and violent weather, and gigantic snowfalls, avalanches, and rock slides altered the topography of its slopes day by day.

The usual route, pioneered by Sir Edmund Hillary, the beekeeper's son from New Zealand, has taken the climbing teams

from their base camps up the Khumbu Glacier, a continent of ice—a labyrinth of broken slabs, frighteningly deep crevasses, monstrous ice towers, and ragged ridges—plunging some 2,000 feet (610 m) down a steep gradient. Beyond the glacier, the route advances through the Western Cwm (coom)—a bowl or amphitheater—at 22,400 feet (6,706 m), and across the Lhotse face. This is a long, steep slope of rock and rock-hard ice rising to 26,000 feet (7,925 m), across from Lhotse itself, the southern peak of Everest. Crossing it, through blasts of the prevailing westerly wind, leads to the South Col, a pass through a ridge, above which lies the summit pyramid. At 29,028 feet (8,848 m) there is the apex and no further to go.

To make it possible for the ultimate climbers to achieve the summit of such mountains requires a tremendous logistical effort. The 1953 expedition that put Hillary and the Nepalese Sherpa Tenzing Norgay atop Everest—the first success in nine attempts—had a roster of twelve climbers, forty Sherpa guides wise in the ways of the great mountains, and seven hundred porters.

Even getting to the base of Everest is a considerable exercise. Food and equipment must be trekked in through the marshy lowlands of the Terai, beyond the headwater tributaries of the Ganges, through paddy fields, rain forest, and alpine meadows, moving past apricot and cherry trees, past rhododendrons, palms, bamboo, and magnolias blooming serenely in the lee of the gigantic range.

The foothills are surmounted, the objective looms. Beyond the main base a succession of camps—way stations—is established, starting perhaps at 19,000 feet (5,791 m). Each has food, shelter, oxygen, medical supplies, extra gear, and each is a stepping stone to supply or resupply the next one, some 2,000 feet higher up the line. The final camp is set up amid the snow and ice at nearly 28,000 feet (8,534 m)—as close as possible for the team that will make the assault on the summit. Along the route the remnants of other encampments are encountered. One expedition, years later, found George Mallory's ice ax, a mute clue to the disappearance of one of Britain's great climbers, who made several assaults on Everest—"Because it is there"—and did not return from the last, in 1924. He was seen headed for the top with a companion, and it is possible that they made it before whatever accident befell them.

Most incredible is the thought of the pair struggling upward at that altitude without oxygen tanks. But that was invariably the case in those days, despite the fact that the air five miles up is almost too thin to sustain human life. In that meager atmosphere climbers are afflicted with anoxia, the mental and physical disturbances that result from insufficient oxygen in the blood. Symptoms are headache, stomach upset, a general feeling of illness, and in extreme cases there can be a fatal pulmonary edema. Because the brain cells are most sensitive to oxygen deprivation, there are also pronounced mental aberrations: forgetfulness, hallucinations, loss of problem-solving ability (a study by scientists at the University of Alaska revealed that three climbers on the Kahiltna Glacier required approximately twice as much time to solve a series of subtraction problems after remaining at 18,000 feet for six days as they did at 7,000 feet), and an inability to report fully and accurately the chronology of one's actions. Climbers operating under such stresses find their energies depleted and judgment impaired even as they face the final challenge of the topmost thousand feet.

Finally, there is weather—capricious, implacable, and, in the Himalayan heights, destructively violent. The spring weeks of the year in which peaks like Everest are climbable are limited at best. Unexpected storms in this period may ruin an expedition's carefully laid plans, abort the effort, and nullify the thousands of dollars and man-hours expended.

Withal, the great peaks *are* climbed. Everest, since the Hillary-Norgay triumph, has had some fifty visitors to its summit representing teams from Switzerland, China, Japan, India, Italy, and the United States. Like all great barriers—like, for instance, the four-minute mile—it seems that once breached they become vulnerable to other assaults.

Eventually, what were once considered difficult climbs become commonplace, and experts searching out new challenges for their skills try alternative routes up familiar peaks. In recent years climbers have achieved the forbidding north wall of the Eiger, the south face of McKinley, even the southwest face of Everest. A British team found a way to negotiate a stratum of rock 500 to 800 feet high that had halted climbers on five earlier expeditions.

There still are numerous unclimbed—and unclimbable—peaks. Hundreds lie within the maze of the Himalayas and the associated systems that thrust into Pakistan, Afghanistan, the Asian wilderness of the Soviet Union, and the little-known reaches of far western China. Many of these are simply too remote geographically to be accessible, while the ranges of the Pamirs, Tien Shan, and Altai are in exotic areas of the Soviet Union and the People's Republic of China, neither of which has been encouraging to visitors. (The USSR, however, began relaxing its restrictions in the mid-1970s, and foreign climbers are now welcome on many Soviet mountains.)

There is considerable curiosity about the mountains of the USSR. Pik Kommunism, formerly named Pik Stalin, is at 24,590 feet (7,495 m) the highest point in the Soviet domain. It lies in the Pamirs of Central Asia, dominating the republics of Kirghizia and Tadzhikistan, and was first ascended in 1933. Nearby, as mountain distances go, is Pik Lenin, third highest Soviet peak at 23,400 feet (7,132 m). It has been climbed frequently, but is still a respectable effort, and a hazardous one when buffeted by hostile mountaintop weather. An experienced climbing team of eight Russian women died in a storm there in 1974.

The complications and expense of Himalayan adventures are not for younger climbing enthusiasts, particularly the increasing number of young Americans who find their challenges in low-altitude climbs of particular difficulty, in simplification of technique, or in the relatively new sport of ice climbing.

Rock climbing, as opposed to mountaineering, began in the 1930s and involves pinnacles, walls, chimneys, cracks—rocks of unimpressive height, but requiring strength, agility, and judgment of a high order. Some require the usual climbing apparatus: carabiners, nuts, chocks, devices that can be wedged into seams in the rock and provide support for the climber. Others are, as far as possible, "clean" climbs, those using the fewest artificial aids and therefore leaving the least evidence of human presence on the skin of the rock. And some are "free" climbs, a hands-and-feet scramble without gear of any kind. It is even possible to find extremely taxing climbs on ten-foot boulders—taxing because they offer little purchase and require tremendous strength in arms, legs, and fingers. "Boulder gymnasts," as they are called, often train by doing one-arm chins on a bar.

Ice climbing is a daredevil sport of recent vintage. It involves finding a more or less vertical wall of ice and climbing it. The most dangerous, and therefore most desirable and exhilarating, vertical is a frozen waterfall. It is ascended with the aid of two ice axes with curved picks (for better holding power) and crampons—spikes strapped to one's shoes.

So how does one become a climber?

The art is taught by qualified mountain guides and instructors. Americans can rely on the personnel in national parks such as Yosemite; Canada's provincial parks also offer instruction. The levels of instruction in North America are considered high. Leading American mountain clubs and colleges have instructors who teach basics.

Cragsmanship is taught in Wales and Scotland, and the British Country Wide Holiday Association has made it a tradition to offer one-week courses in various parts of England and Scotland.

Some of the best instruction in the United States is available from mountaineering clubs. The Colorado Mountain Club, for example, organizes special courses for adults as well as for teen-agers. The program begins with lectures and films plus an indoor demonstration, followed by practice sessions on nearby mountains. Later the club's volunteer teachers take students on actual climbs. Rock scaling is part of the program of several Outward Bound camps for teen-agers. A number of mountaineering guide services offer instruction ranging from a day to a full week at reasonable rates.

Proper position is all. New climbers often lean *into* the mountain, hugging it. Experts know that it is better to keep the upper body *away* from the rock. They lean out and look up. They develop an easy climbing rhythm, almost like runners or skiers. To move upward between two vertical slabs, one makes a wedge of the human anatomy with back and leg pressure. This is called "chimneying."

Rock climbing is less an acrobatic act than a sport for the well-conditioned and the intelligent. A wall can involve the mind like a chess game. The student learns to study a rock face from level ground and on the way up. Bill Forrest, an American inventor of climbing aids, says, "Look with the fingers and feet as well as with the eyes." You must scrutinize a wall and choose each foot- and handhold with care. You learn to test rock. Will it hold? Could it crumble? Is that crack too high up to be reached? Even on easier pitches, good climbers make it a habit to pick their steps with deliberation. No haste. No slipping. No falling. The elements of balance are important. A climber always tries to have three points of contact with the rock. The contact can be two hands and one foot, or one hand and two feet. Knees are never used. Nor do skilled cragsmen grip bushes, small trees, or other "vegetable holds." Plants seldom grow deep roots in rocky country and are likely to pull free under a climber's weight.

The instructor's introduction of a climbing rope heralds "technical climbing." Modern synthetic ropes—nylon or Perlon —are sturdy, resilient, durable. (An 11-mm German Perlon rope can actually hold some four thousand pounds before it breaks.) Colors abound. You see bright reds, greens, candy stripes. The most popular ropes measure 150 feet, ideal for an average rock-climbing party.

Novices are told immediately to treat their ropes with care. A climbing rope has only a limited span of mountain life. Abuse and abrasion cause the synthetic fibers to weaken and break. One brand actually comes with a label that reads: "If anyone steps on it, even your best friend, bash him!"

For safety's sake it is advisable never to buy a used rope, even if the price seems seductive. Two young Salt Lake City climbers saw a classified ad offering a 150-foot rope for a mere ten dollars. The owner said he had bought it some years ago, but discovered that he preferred hiking to mountaineering. The young climbers bought the rope and rushed off to the towers of Utah's Wasatch Range. They went up smoothly without straining the rope. By noon, in fine sunshine, they reached the top of a tower. Rappel! One boy sat down to assist his descending companion. Before stepping out from his summit perch, the teen-ager took the precaution of testing the nylon, giving it an energetic tug. This was fortunate. The rope tore halfway through, almost like packing twine. It later turned out that the former owner had stored the rope in the ruinous heat and humidity of his basement for several years.

A rope is vital for several basic rock-climbing maneuvers. The first is the "static" belay, a stance that guarantees another person's safety while he is moving up or down a rock. A belayer should be well anchored to a rock or strong tree, so that he controls the rope to climbers below and is totally secure, no mat-

101

*Rock-climbing gear includes
(top) well-tested line, various
pitons (wedges), carabiners (snap-links),
foxhead nuts (bottom l), and
crampon (bottom r) for walking ice.*

ter what happens. Additional security can be achieved if the belayer positions himself with legs propped against a rock. One can learn the static belay in a few lessons. The "dynamic" belay, which secures the leader from below, is trickier. It involves the placement of hardware by the leader as he moves up a wall.

The second rope-climbing essential is the "rappel," known in Europe as *abseil*. It allows a person to back down even the steepest mountain face swiftly. The rope, arms, and hands must be in the correct position before a rappeler can brave the void. The first step into the abyss can trouble beginners. If a student hesitates on the edge and can't work up the nerve, the instructor may talk him into trying: "You're on belay. Just lean back and out." After a hesitant few feet, most students make it down the entire wall.

Under certain circumstances the rappel can become a dangerous maneuver, especially for tyros, but even for experts in bad weather. In some cases new climbers set out with too short a rope. One such mishap occurred on the Third Flatiron, just outside Boulder, Colorado. The exact locale was a rappel that goes by the fine name of "Friday's Folly." Actors: three university freshmen, only one of whom had rappeled before. The first one did well enough on the 127-foot rappel with 120 feet of nylon. When he reached the end he let himself down to the very tip, and dropped elegantly to the slabs below. So did the number-two man. The third fellow, however, hadn't been briefed. Suddenly he had no rope,

and just as suddenly he fell, breaking a leg and three ribs. A rappel into fog-shrouded or unknown territory also can create a tricky situation, even for otherwise competent mountaineers.

One of the strangest short-rope cases occurred on an Austrian tower. Threatened by lightning, the climbers had to get down as fast as possible. They picked the shortest of several possible routes. They'd never done it before, and unfortunately they couldn't see if there was a platform at the end of the rappel rope. The first climber went down. He did well until he bumped into an overhang. He had now to continue without assistance from his feet. This is called a "free" rappel. Expert that he was, the man kept his body parallel to the rope and continued his downward journey. All at once he was out of rope. He hung ten meters from a narrow ledge which, however, was not directly in his fall line. Worse, the wind and the rope were twirling him around his own axis! What to do? He tried swinging toward the rock, with the idea of climbing up again. But the rope cut into his chest and kept him from breathing. The attempt failed. After painful hours the climbers found a solution. They strung together a number of short sling ropes. When the life line was still not long enough, they used the belts from their trousers. Only in this manner did they finally reach bottom. Some terrain knowledge and a longer rope would have helped!

Cragsmen must also learn to adopt a code of standard calls. A climber who

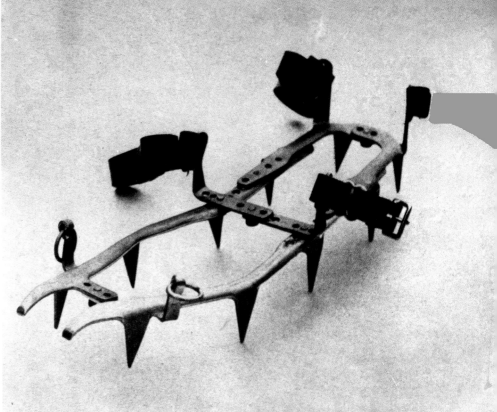

*Plain & Fancy: Young man below
performs a standard rappel.
Experts (r) cluster on Yosemite's Lost
Arrow spire. Note climber on
pinnacle's outside edge.*

touches bottom after a rappel, for instance, should call, "Off rappel!" The next climber can then start down. "On belay" means that a belayer is secure. When someone wants to start uphill, the correct call is "Climbing!" The shout "Tension!" signifies a request for a tighter rope, which helps give support in an emergency. "Slack!" asks for a looser line. Such signals become especially important when there are 100-foot distances between two people, as for instance, on a long pitch that cannot be totally viewed from the top, or on a lengthy descent, when someone will be out of sight. A climber can warn those below about a dislodged rock by yelling "Rock!" If someone actually starts to fall, the climber must yell, "Falling!" (A competent belay won't permit a long fall, and should stop the plunge soon enough.)

Calls should be made in a clear, loud voice, parade-ground fashion. A new instructor once directed two even less experienced friends on a cliff in Wales. The leader called out an order to one man too gently. The other man thought that the instructor meant *him*. He reached up the holdless rock and fell like a wingless dove. Fortunately, he was well belayed.

A climber cannot change the code.

The scene is Mount Washington, New Hampshire. An elderly European is stranded just below the icy summit. He has been climbing alone, and now he can go neither up nor down. The time is 2:00 P.M., and just to the west a young climbing group bursts into sight. The old man's heart leaps. At the top of his voice, he calls, "Hello!" The leader, a young New Hampshire lad, hears the call and stops in his tracks. Listens again. "Hello!" The young leader turns to his companions. "He must be greeting us!" Politely, he calls back, "Hello!" and continues the journey with his two friends.

Trembling, the European sees the group disappear behind a crest. Why did they leave him? Suddenly he understands. He'd merely shouted a greeting. Now they're already out of hearing. But all's well that ends well. He finally called, "Help! Help!" The climbers heard the shouts on their way down and rescued him.

Accidents occur because a beginner climbs alone. At one of the national parks, rangers figure that it costs about $10,000 a year in overtime wages to assist stranded, or hurt, solo adventurers. (In some parks climbing alone is prohibited.)

A distinguished British mountaineer once took a plunge that resulted in several leg operations and a lifelong limp. The accident made him ponder the wisdom of solo climbing. "I wanted freedom from the ropes and from the team," wrote the late Sir Arnold Lunn. "I wanted to be alone in Wales. Suddenly a rock swayed. It gave, and I was falling. A first somersault . . . I saw the mountain upside down. Then I hit a ledge, and another ledge. I thought, this is enough! But it wasn't! It took eight hours to find and rescue me."

*Setting up a hanging bivouac.
Two climbers (one already reclining
in his hammock) and their gear
will hang from single anchor
overnight, resume climb next day.*

Just how dangerous is mountaineering?

Every climber faces what are known as "objective" dangers—rock slides, bad weather, avalanches. While a group has little control over a force majeure, the lone climber is even worse off. What if a falling boulder should crush his leg? Who helps him off the mountain? What about the person who never tells anyone what his climbing destination is?

Risks naturally decrease for the prudent, a fact borne out by the accident reports turned in to the American Alpine Club. In a typical year, only about two hundred and fifty North Americans are involved in major climbing mishaps. Of these, there are about one hundred fatalities. Analysis shows that eighty percent of the accidents are caused by human failings: lack of experience, exceeding one's abilities, climbing when exhausted, pushing on in bad weather, running out of food, climbing in unknown terrain without preparation. No one should ignore the threat of storms in the Rockies, particularly in the Tetons. The south and middle Tetons can be as socked in as the 13,766-foot (4,196-m) Grand Teton. Periodic clouds make it impossible to see the Grand's granite slabs, chock stones, chimneys, and unmelted snows. Progress slows. During most months Teton mornings are chilly, afternoons mostly rainy. A winter ascent is madness, especially without arctic equipment. The Grand's winter weather is notoriously severe.

The objective dangers of blizzards increase for a fatigued party. One group set out into a national forest, driving a full night and climbing an entire day. By 6:00 P.M. the sky was black. Thick clouds rumbled across the crest. Yet the climbers, tired to the marrow, pushed up. At 7:00 P.M. they reached the hard snow under the summit. The cold stung their faces, seeped through their pants, crept into their parkas. Their feet felt like lead. But they kept on climbing until a disastrous fall stopped them, and they had to be rescued.

In many such cases, individuals are overconfident and get in over their heads. Rescue figures for North America and Europe are staggering. Each summer some two hundred people must be plucked from mountains near Banff by rescue teams. Amateur climbers simply are not up to the difficulties. One can multiply this single resort's statistic several hundred times.

Some individuals get into trouble because they climb without equipment. A typical illustration: it is a summer morning on the Hudson shores, in New York State. A college student wants to impress his girl friend. He takes her to one of the most popular rock faces. Of these, the uppermost tower is the most difficult. One can reach it by some winding forest trails, and the collegian and his friend are hiking upward through the sun. Suddenly he announces that he'd like to try the highest, hairiest tower. Without a rope.

He positions the girl below, where she can admire him. He has done some rock scrambling before, and up he goes, all show. After about thirty feet he gets stuck. For

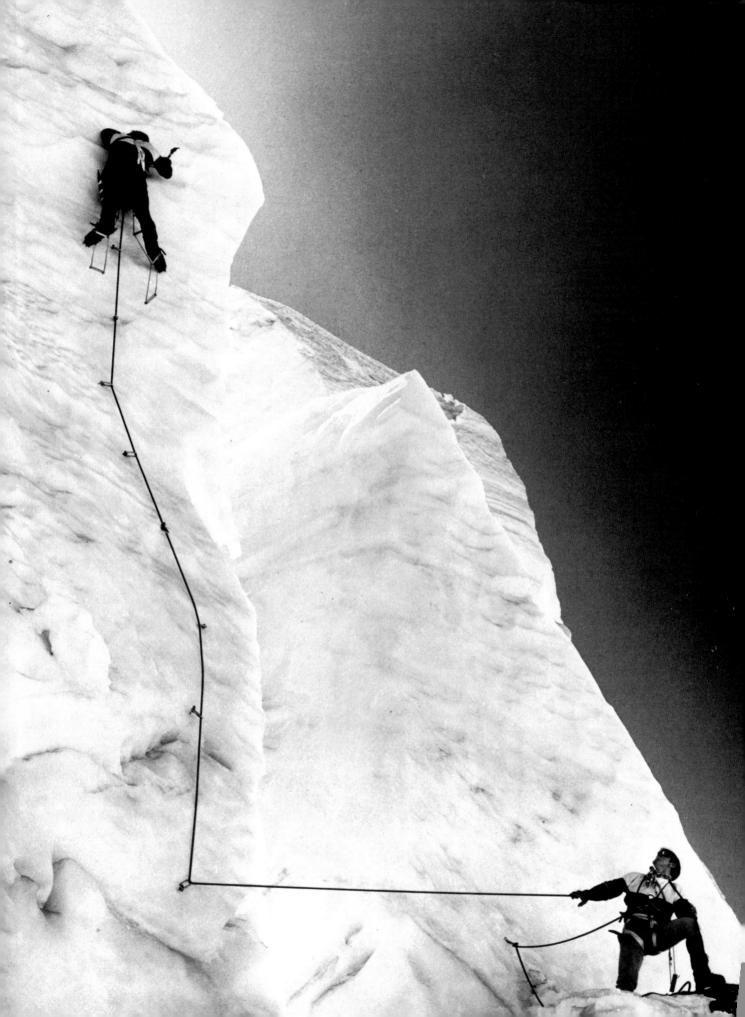

*Ice climbing is a daredevil
sport requiring only vertical ice
—preferably a frozen waterfall—
which one ascends with ice
ax and crampon spikes.*

about an hour he can move neither up nor down. There are no possible traverses. He finds himself at his wit's end.

"I'll go for help!" the girl calls to him. But at the same moment, he loses his footing. Fortunately, there is a strong tree a few yards below him and he manages to hold on and then stand on a narrow ledge until someone can come and get him. This is not an unusual case. Every summer rescue groups work day and night, using ropes to help unequipped novices reach safe ground.

Climbing wisdom begins with footwear. For the most severe walls, elite rock climbers use a thin ballet-style shoe, sometimes known as the "friction shoe." Average rock-climbing boots are five to seven inches high, with hard, stiff soles, and tough lugs. They are more efficient than the old-style boots whose hobnails clattered in the streets, made a racket on the rocks, and added unnecessary weight. Sporting-goods shops or specialty stores sell many brands of long-wearing, reasonably priced footwear that makes molehills out of mountains. When buying a pair, be sure to allow enough space for heavy woolen socks. The instep should fit snugly, yet one must have enough room for toe movement. Lack of circulation results in cold feet.

How about clothing? Experience has shown that it's better to be over-equipped than underequipped for high mountains. In some regions a climb can be sufficiently difficult, and the weather sufficiently changeable, for a party to be "benighted," forced to spend the night outdoors. Mountain nights are cold and one welcomes every thread of clothing. This includes adequate outerwear, such as a waterproof poncho for rainy areas, and a well-constructed parka. (A down filling is necessary for high altitudes.)

Cold regions—or the threat of cold—require a different wardrobe. Several layers of clothing give the most protection. For chilly days experts suggest mesh-net underwear, a wool turtleneck, and rugged, nonconstricting pants of inexpensive whipcord or corduroy. Knickers are still popular. Many young people climb in jeans. An unexpected change of weather may have serious consequences. A classic case concerns a young couple—both in shorts—who tried for the top of Mount Washington in midsummer; they died near the summit. The cold was too much for their inadequate clothes. Short-sleeved shirts and thin summer pants can result in frostbite or death in the Alps, too. The victims are often competent climbers. Unfortunately, not even an Everest champion could survive a wet forty-eight hours at 14,000 in shorts.

One summer a large group of middle-aged people tried to pit themselves against the Grand Teton. They wore light windbreakers and thin pants. They brought no goggles. Their food supplies consisted of bread, crackers, some jam, and a can of pineapple. Leadership? Instead of employing a guide, they were led by a hiker who had no knowledge of the climbing route and who made several mistakes. It could have been sunny. But the mountain showed its most evil mood, displaying the worst Wyoming weather. The benighted Teton excursionists found themselves stranded on a ledge. The air turned frigid at night.

Their ordeal lasted seventy-two hours, claimed one fatality, scared everyone, and ruined what could have been a nice trip. Hard hats against falling rocks or ice, sleeping bags, tents, all would have come in handy.

Depending on the steepness and length of a rock climb, the leader brings an assortment of nylon slings, various lengths of rope, and hardware. This will include rock anchors, such as pitons, metal spikes with an eyelet through which a rope can be run; nuts (or chocks), which are placed in cracks and jammed into place by the downward pull of weight; and bolts, which can be hammered into rock that offers no cracks or seams. Anchors can support more than a ton of weight, yet are easily pulled out of lodgments. Aside from the economy involved in retrieving hardware, there is the matter of mountain aesthetics to be considered. Many climbers feel that rusting metal pitons abandoned along the route of a climb are an eyesore, and prefer easily removable nuts or chocks.

The leader also will carry carabiners which can be attached to anchors to guide and secure a running rope. Even experts are only as good as their hardware, and a defective carabiner can be deadly. One of the most tragic losses occurred to the Dave Roberts expe-dition on remote Mount Huntington, Alaska.

On a July night Roberts and Ed Bernd were descending the peak's west face. Two other climbers were in a higher camp. A few minutes before midnight, in the gloomy darkness, Bernd clipped a carabiner into a piton. He slipped the climbing rope into the carabiner, got into a rappel position, and leaned back. Suddenly he was flying through the air. Without a word, he fell 50 feet, hit a steep ice gully, rolled and bounced down another sickening 200 feet. Then he was out of sight. Roberts knew from route photos there would be no stopping until Bernd hit the Tolositna Glacier, 4,000 feet below. A near-vertical fall. Not a chance for survival.

All this happened because Bernd had not inspected his hardware. According to a subsequent investigation by a mountaineering club, "the carabiner was defective. The gate never closed, allowing the carabiner to flip loose."

A novice is not likely to join a Mount Huntington expedition. But hazards exist even close to home. A tyro may get into trouble by attempting a peak that is too difficult. In some cases a newcomer with minimal experience asks to join advanced cragsmen who are headed for a hairy wall.

How does a person know in advance what to expect? And how can the climber tell if he or she has enough ability to handle the situation? The answer is simple. Most rock climbs have been inspected and graded by a mountain club, a guide service, or a climbing party. A regional guidebook may list the grade of difficulty. Forest or park rangers, gendarmeries, rescue services, mountain club files, or the bulletin board of a climbing school should yield information, too. The rock evaluation system applies to both North American and British climbing—in fact, to climbing all over the world, with only slight variations.

Here are the classifications:

Class I: Walking upright.

Class II: Rock scrambling. Proper footgear and use of hands for balance required.

Class III: Climbing steeper ground and rocks. Proper technique required. Exposure not sufficient for a rope.

Class IV: Higher and steeper walls with gradients from 60 degrees to nearly vertical. Ropes required. Chocks or pitons needed to anchor belayer. Some difficulty to be expected.

Class V: More vertical, and even more difficult routes. More hardware, too. Leader moves with extreme caution. (The two climbers at the beginning of this chapter handled a Class V wall.) The British rate Class V as "severe."

Class VI: Climbing where holds or cracks in the rock are not adequate, additional hardware and stirrups (or "etriers") are needed.

Practice and experience in all kinds of terrain contribute to an individual's confidence. The ambitious Class V climber gradually advances to Class VI. At this point, first-rate leadership, talent, good health, self-confidence, and endurance become essential. The climber should be accustomed to "exposure" to steep drop-offs. Raw courage, mechanical aptitude, a sense for route finding, along with weather knowledge, now pay off.

The elite climber must be tough in many respects. He may attempt vertical ventures that demand several days using the techniques described here. Such a climb can involve one or more nights in a hammock suspended over a precipice. Stamina plays a big role, too. Certain weather problems may result in day climbs lasting ten to fifteen hours. If a roped climber takes a long fall, it could mean a setback and undermine self-confidence. Yvon Chouinard, one of America's leading rock experts, actually fell for about 160 feet in the Tetons. "It took three years of steady climbing to regain my confidence," Chouinard recalls. "Each climb during those years was a battle against myself and my fears." Chouinard first saw the Yosemite peaks on a moonlit night, and his disbelief ("I had never seen such walls!") fired up his earlier enthusiasm. Then he went on his first Yosemite overnight bivouac, a "cold, frightening, uncomfortable experience," followed by another fifteen nights on the rocks. "All ordeals." Chouinard eventually achieved international stature as a climber regaining his confidence. The same is true for many other mountaineers. They battle hard to keep their cool. They see advanced mountaineering as an

113

opportunity to achieve perfect self-control.

Advanced rockmanship involves surmounting outcrops known as overhangs. Such severe obstacles call for extra pitons and rope ladders. In fact, certain overhangs leave the climber little choice but to use more gear for safety's sake. "Direct aid," also known as "artificial" climbing, becomes the only method when life is at stake on nearly holdless walls and overhangs with 2,000-foot chasms below.

To a few of these ace climbers a regular job, marriage, family life, even studies, all become taboo. Only rock climbing counts. A well-known young Scots mountaineer actually lived off unemployment checks, so that he could devote himself to his passion. To get his check, however, he had to report once a week to the Glasgow employment authorities. The climber begrudged them that one day

*Exploratory Descent: Rappel
drops climber into dim, cool depths
of a glacial crevasse. Risk
is slight under these conditions,
but ascent will be slower.*

and complained to his friends that the officials "had tried to fix him up" with steady work! Some "climbing bums" live off their indulgent families or girl friends. A few combine their hunger for the rock with seasonal employment at climbing schools, or as guides. They admittedly have their best time off the job, however. Their climbing prowess is legendary.

Most of today's best international cragsmen are less than twenty-five years old, and many are under twenty. These Class V and VI rock artists are extraordinarily knowledgeable, skillful, agile, and safety-conscious. Thanks to better training and equipment they scale cliffs that would have been considered impossible twenty years ago. The young climbers perform rock feats almost casually. They push back climbing barriers in narrow Colorado canyons, on the domes of Yosemite, among the Scots cliffs.

They gravitate only to the most forbidding rock structures, to sheer enormous walls. A super-mountaineer is like a medieval warrior assaulting impossible citadels. On guard! Watch those battlements! Unexpected bombardment of loose rock. Booms of invisible cannons. Go back, soldier! A snowslide's air blast is enough to sweep a climber into the depths. Some daring lifelong climbers are lucky. They move on and up the fortress, despite the counterforces.

The moody mountain often spares a life, letting the attacker limp away. But the ungrateful human vows to return. An Italian named Claudio Corti has defied the Tre Cime of the Dolomites. He had conquered most of the Alps when he found himself stranded on a Swiss peak. Corti was stuck for seven days. His water ran out and he got so thirsty that, half mad, he bit into the ice, losing several teeth. He never reached the top. When he was finally down in the village again, Corti shook his fist at the 6,000-foot heap of frozen stone and snow. "This time the mountains got me!" he raged. "Next time I'll get the mountain!"

The next time was a year later. The Italian climber was promptly hit by an ice block. When he came to, his face looked a bleeding mess. A friend leaned over the man. "*Povero Claudio,*" he said with sympathy. Corti wiped the blood away, and got weakly to his feet. "Poor nothing! When do we start again?"

He eventually defeated the adversary.

The annals of mountaineering contain many accounts of die-hards returning three, four, six times, until they finally triumph over the peak. When at last they stand on the summit, older men may hug each other, or be moved to tears. "I was born all over again!" Gaston Rébuffat said of one first summit ascent. "I felt nothing but rapture!" said Maurice Herzog about the chilly summit of Annapurna.

The rapture for most people stems not only from the conquest of a mountain, but the conquest of the self. They mustered the strength, the stamina, the control of all fears, and made the top.

5

Mountain People
and Their Communities

*Preceding pages: At 12,000 ft
(3,658 m) elevation,
Quechua Indians of Bolivia
gather for village festival.
Above: Nearly noon on
a bright, clear day in the
scenic farm- and dairylands
of Austria's Vorarlberg.*

120

At least ninety percent of the world's people live at elevations of less than 2,000 feet. This is not surprising, for to man, mountain country is less hospitable than are lowlands. Remote high places are difficult for man to inhabit for the same reasons they are limiting to flora and fauna: mountains are cold, have less oxygen, and are steep, which in man's case not only makes it harder to move about but also to find places to build, grow crops, and raise livestock. Still another dimension: man is basically social, thriving on companionship and making his progress by interacting with fellow men, sharing goods and experience. Mountain people are isolated from the mainstreams of civilization. Their survival often depends less on other men than on successful confrontations with nature. The true alpine dwellers, like their plant and animal counterparts, are distinctly different from those living in the lowlands. They are not the same as lowlanders either physically or psychologically.

Mountain people also differ socially from those of the flatlands, but in many instances these differences have been the result only of geography, with mountains ranking among the last domains of ethnic regionalism. Mountaineers of the North American Appalachians, the Highlanders of Scotland—distinctive ways of life and dialects have identified mountain people. But many of these mountains are comparatively low, and the unique customs and language of these people fade when their world is touched by modern transportation and communication. With the mountains no longer a barrier, their people are soon absorbed almost indistinguishably into the meld of humanity. True, some of them cling to the old ways—but less so than in times past. They no longer look upon all lowlanders as foreigners, for they have become a part of the greater world themselves, the interflow and amalgamation leveling the humanity though the mountains themselves remain much the same and may hold their people forever, at least in spirit. Few who are born of the mountains can ever escape them totally.

But there are also places in the world where mountain people have been affected only slightly by the modern world and where, as a result of countless generations of life at high altitudes, the people themselves are not like lowlanders even physically. These are the inhabitants of the highest mountain ranges in the world: the Himalayas of Asia and the Andes of South America.

An adult Himalayan villager's heart may weigh 350 grams, about twenty-five percent more than the heart of an Indian flatlander. The composition of the mountain man's blood is different, too, containing as much as twenty percent more red blood corpuscles than the blood of a lowlander. Still another difference, he has a bigger chest, in which he accommodates larger lungs and consequently exposes more capillaries to receive oxygen in respiration. In body proportion, these mountain people tend to be short and stocky, hence the blood does not have to be pumped as far. All of these are adaptations that permit the mountain man to take in a greater volume of the rarefied air, to

extract from it as much oxygen as possible, and to move it through his body with a more powerful pump. His fingers and toes, the extremities most vulnerable to frostbite, are enriched with capillaries to help keep them warm. A true alpine man thinks nothing of walking through the snow barefoot.

Visitors to Nepal are always startled by the physical strength and hardiness of the mountain-bred Sherpas. Their endurance is legendary. Both men and women regularly walk more than twenty miles a day, with much of the mileage uphill. The porters serving mountain expeditions carry loads weighing as much as a hundred pounds (although forty is normal). They trudge ahead at a constant pace, neither too fast nor too slow. They make few stops, for a pause breaks the rhythm. American trekkers compare their legs to hydraulic jacks or pistons. Even if a loadless client attempts to

Brawny, tireless Nepalese Sherpas
tote supplies in high country en route
to Everest. Normal load is 40 pounds.
In background looms
Chomo Lonzo (25,640 ft/7,815 m).

walk faster, these heavily loaded mountain men manage to stay ahead, all the while smiling as though totally refreshed. Their bare feet are callused, their necks massive from years of carrying heavy loads.

Actually, it is unfair and even inaccurate to generalize in comparing the stamina of these true mountain dwellers with that of lowlanders, for almost invariably it is a comparison of the lowlander with the mountain man in the latter's environment. What the mountain man can do is really not remarkable or even a matter of coping with difficult conditions as far as he is concerned. He performs without discomfort because he is physically adapted for high-altitude living, as fit at 19,000 feet as a lowlander is at sea level. Taken to the low country, the mountain man becomes uncomfortable and quickly fatigued, unable to match the lowlander. The physical differences

123

Machu Picchu, marvelously intact fortress city of the ancient Incas of Peru, lies in a narrow saddle between two cloud-wrapped peaks of the Andes, 8,000 ft (2,438 m) up.

are indeed that pronounced.

Psychologists note that these people of the high country also differ considerably in attitude from those who live in lowlands. Man's impression of his own importance is affected by the awesome presence of peaks rising to 20,000 feet and higher. Isolation results in self-reliance and self-sufficiency. In the mountain kingdom of Nepal, rimmed on the north by the mightiest mountains in the world, a highland farmer often lives some distance from any neighbor. He owns a plot of stony ground that he has terraced for growing wheat, and he tills with a crude plow that breaks down often. Perhaps he also raises a few chickens. The Nepali has neither frills nor money. He is a frontiersman of sorts, but his frontier is not likely to change no matter how hard he works it.

The Himalayan people are surrounded by stunning scenery. Mysticism and religion show a strong influence. Muslims and Hindus predominate, but remember that Buddha was born in Rummindei, a town located in what is now Nepal. In the highlands, Buddhist prayer wheels turn, prayer flags snap, and the haunting musical instruments of Buddhist priests can be heard.

At 12,715 feet (3,875 m), the Buddhist monastery at Thyangboche is one of the most compelling sights in the mountains. It rises level upon level to a gold-crowned temple starkly outlined against the masses of rock, ice, and sky. Here in view of three Himalayan giants—Everest, Nhupse, and Lhotse—are the lamas in their robes or, on special occasions, in

125

*Camels, goats, and other livestock
are watered at oasis in Aïr Mountains
of northern Niger. Aïrs are one
of three massifs afloat in
vast sandy sea of the Sahara.*

red-and-yellow silk costumes. Oil lamps flickering against old beams illuminate the monks, and there are ancient altars, statues of Buddha, scrolls, and murals depicting bears, leopards, dragons, and demons. Long remembered by the visitor are the sounds of cymbals and gongs and the discordant music of the long copper trumpets. This monastery in the mountains transports the traveler to another world.

The architecture of these religious outposts varies in the different Himalayan countries. Some of the monasteries have exquisitely arched pagodalike roofs. The isolated, balconied monasteries near Darjeeling in India are among the world's most graceful. Other handsome lamasaries can be reached only by stone staircases that zigzag like the lofty peaks themselves.

A multiplicity of ethnic groups inhabits the globe's highest range, where the high mountains running east and west are divided into isolated domains by great gorges and blocks of mountains. Herbert Tichy, an Austrian explorer, counted no fewer than eighteen tribes in one small section of the northeastern Himalayas south of the Chinese border and east of Bhutan. Intrigued by these little-known groups and the scant records even of their existence, he observed that "each tribe had its own language. It was an almost hopeless proposition for the ethnologist." Among the tribes whose distinct character has been molded by isolation are the Mishmi, who eat live beetles and worms; the Balti; and the Champa. Some of the tribes are nomadic. The Bhatias, for example,

move with the seasons. Using sheep and goats as pack animals, they transport rice and other grains from the highland fields to barter for salt or trinkets in the lowlands.

Gurkhas, also of Mongoloid extraction and predominantly of the Hindu faith, are perhaps the best known of all the Nepalese people. Gurkha was the name of a family that ruled the Nepalese in the mid-1700s. They originated in a province of Nepal and were members of a military caste, the Rajputs. To this day, the Gurkha tribe provides most of Nepal's professional soldiers. About 250,000 of these mountain mercenaries fought on the side of the British during World War II, and some of them still serve in the British army. The Gurkha's best-known weapon is the *kukri*, a short sword with a wickedly curved blade.

The Pathans, of the heights of Afghanistan and northern Pakistan, are also famous as warriors, but martial people are the exception in the Himalayas. Most of the groups favor farming or are pastoral, bringing their flocks of sheep and goats to lower elevations when their mountain pastures turn white with winter snow, and going back to the heights as soon as they become green in summer. The farmers do well, for the Himalayas abound in tillable land. Potatoes grow even at 14,000 feet in Nepal. Fine crops of corn, wheat, rice, oats, and millet are produced at lower elevations, and tea thrives as high as 4,000 feet.

High in the Karakoram range, stretching across Pakistan's northern border, the mountains providing almost total isolation,

is the fabled valley of the Hunzukuts. Here in the mountains are fertile fields of wheat and barley, orchards and vineyards, and gardens yielding a wide variety of vegetables. Twenty kinds of apricots are grown in the valley. The mountain people stay healthy on a diet of milk, cheese, bread, raw fruits, and vegetables. Meat is scarce. The air is superbly fresh, the mountain water pure. Visitors are rarely allowed in the Princedom of Hunza, and so this "lost kingdom of the Himalayas" has remained virtually unchanged through the ages. Burushaski, the

Hunzukuts' unique language, has no known relationship to any other tongue in the world, so that speech as well as the mountain isolation is a barrier to outside influences. Like other mountain people, the Hunzukuts are noted for their endurance. One Hunza messenger allegedly ran 280 miles in seven days, crossing several high mountain passes and fording turbulent rivers. These fair-skinned people are known also for their longevity, for Hunza is among the few places in the world with a statistically significant number of centenarians. Gerontologists be-

*Elevations have always inspired
reverence—nowhere more quaintly than at
Le Puy, in south-central France,
where the tiny church of St. Michel
d'Aiguille perches atop sugarloaf.*

lieve that the genetic strain for long life passed to these people by their forebears has remained pure because of their isolation. For whatever significance it might have, the mountains do seem to contribute to a long life. Some five thousand people over a hundred years old live in the Caucasus range of Russia, and an even higher concentration of superbly healthy and fit individuals lives in the USSR's mountainous Abkhazian region.

A disproportionately large number of centenarians is found also in the South American Andes, and the good health of these people has aroused the interest of physicians. The oldest are Indians of Ecuador, concentrated in Vilcabamba and nearby villages. Many exceed the age of 130, and some have lived past 140, usually slipping away quietly in their sleep rather than succumbing to illness. Typically the men live longer than the women, and often a man will have several wives, some of whom are a quarter of a century or more younger than he is. Even the older Vilcabambans toil in the fields all day and then enjoy a robust sex life at night.

Dr. David Davies, a leading British gerontologist, spent several years investigating these mountain people. "Walking up the steep slopes increases the efficiency of their hearts," he reported. In addition to genetics, lack of stress and their diet (principally fish and fruit) are factors in the Vilcabambans' longevity. The mountain environment? Dr. Davies, after interviewing many mountain people in the Andes as well as in other parts of the world, concludes that mountain living does indeed contribute to longevity. Most of the centenarians, according to his research, live at altitudes between 5,700 and 6,300 feet (1,737–1,920 m).

Many of the Andean people, of course, live far above the heights that lowlanders can tolerate in comfort. Indians of Chile work in mines at 18,000 feet and still function well. In Bolivia, the population is centered in the *altiplano*, or highland plateaus. The city of La Paz is located at 12,000 feet (3,658 m), Potosí at 13,000. Miners, farmers, herdsmen, and other laborers go much higher in the mountains to work. The Indians plow a poor soil and plant their crops in a hostile climate, yet some Peruvian potato farmers eke out their livelihood at 14,000 feet. Their plots of land can be incredibly small, and if the Indian serves a large landowner, his pay is pitiful. Many Andeans sweat in the copper, tin, and silver mines that stud the high mountains. On the lower Chilean and Argentinian slopes, where the soil is both more plentiful and more fertile, living conditions seem better. And everywhere in the Andes, as if to compensate for the hardships, people favor brightly colored and boldly patterned clothing, and joyous religious festivals are an important part of life.

Most Andean Indians are descendants of the proud Incas, the most famous of South America's pre-Columbian cultures and the continent's leading power in the fifteenth century. Interestingly, the Incas are related through millennia of generations to their mountain brethren in the Himalayas, sharing

129

*Preceding pages: Cowboys move
a herd of white-faced Herefords
through upland ranges of
the Continental Divide, near
West Yellowstone, Montana.*

with them a heritage of Mongolian stock. The Incas' closest relatives today include the Quechua, known as the "warm valley people," and the Aymaras. Both groups live in the high mountains of Bolivia and Peru, in much the same manner as their ancestors. Historians speculate that the inaccessible valleys have helped to preserve ancient ways, and just as these mountain Indians differ from their brothers on the coast, differences also often exist from one valley to the next. Some tribes seem gregarious; others keep to themselves.

Hidden high in the mountains, the Peruvian citadel of Machu Picchu escaped the gold-lusty Spanish conquerors of the sixteenth century, its location lost even to people of the Andes until it was rediscovered in 1911 by Hiram Bingham, an American archeologist. Machu Picchu, the "lost city of the Incas," was built by Manco II, one of the last of the Inca rulers. When the Incas were overcome by the Spaniards, the Spanish conqueror Pizarro made Manco their leader. This was fitting, because Manco was the grandson of Huyana, one of the greatest of the Inca rulers. Pizarro expected Manco to be a puppet, but Manco was young, ambitious, and rebellious. Taking some of his people with him, he fled to the Cordillera de Vilcabamba, one of the most inaccessible areas of the Andes. It was here that Manco built his new city, a high fortress from which he could harass the Spaniards and which, because of its altitude, the Spaniards could not storm.

But already the great Inca empire, which once extended almost the length of the Andes, was doomed. Year by year, by trickery, by direct battle, and by sheer numbers, the Incas were subdued until nothing remained of the once powerful nation but the ruins of their buildings. Lost to the world for centuries was the location of Machu Picchu, the last of their strongholds.

Hiram Bingham found Machu Picchu nearly intact, almost 8,000 feet above sea level and situated on a steep, 2,000-foot ridge overlooking a canyon. A marvel of masonry, it is built of giant blocks of stone cut from the mountains and fitted together so skillfully that they have stayed in place for centuries, withstanding even the earthquakes that sometimes shake the region. No mortar holds them together, only snug-fitting, complicated, well-engineered angles. The stone houses, temples, and towers are connected by an intricate system of staircases. Archeologists later discovered aqueducts, baths, fountains, religious shrines, weapons, tools, and pottery. Today Machu Picchu is an important tourist attraction, accessible by train and complete with guided tours and a hotel for travelers.

Just sixty-seven miles from Machu Picchu is Cuzco, a modern Peruvian metropolis. This was the original Inca capital, and the ancient walls and foundations still stand, along with the churches of the Spanish conquistadors.

To this day, native Andean villagers, like many mountain people, pluck building materials from the nearest slopes. The Incas used stone; present-day natives commonly

132

shape a mixture of mud and straw into adobe bricks. Roofs can be covered with shingles, pebbles, logs, boulders, or straw. All of these materials contribute to the picture of the community and its people.

Mountain people may live a simple life, but it can also be a cheerful one. One might consider the Basques who herd sheep in the western U.S. Rockies or hold their lone vigils in the sometimes foggy Pyrenees that separate Spain from France. The Basques' ethnic origins remain unclear, but they seem to have been in Europe longer than other groups. Some anthropologists theorize that these dark-complexioned mountain people may have migrated to the Iberian peninsula from the Caucasus some two thousand years before Christ. The Basque sheepherders and farmers wear the berets and the modest working clothes of their ancestors. They live simply and accept their place in the mountain world. Bernard De Voto once asked a Basque why he chose to live among sheep. "I seek the quiet heart," the shepherd answered.

The "quiet heart" of solitude can be found by the Basques among the meadows and knolls of their homeland and on the hillsides of Nevada, Idaho, Colorado, and Wyoming. The sheepherders are in tune with their mountains, which make (as they like to explain) a "mighty big bedroom." Most of the herds are owned by older Basque men, who let the younger, unmarried men do the herding while they themselves tend to family life. For the young sheepherders, the annual shearing and its accompanying festival, with dancing, weight lifting, and wine drinking, seems to fulfill much of the need for entertainment. Whether living in the United States, France, or Spain, Basques hold on to their difficult-to-learn language. It resembles none other in Europe and still puzzles philologists.

Just as the high mountains shape men's bodies, making them better able to endure the rigors of their environment, so the mountains mold men's minds, giving them a perspective and psychological make-up that seems peculiar to peak living. With few exceptions, the people of high places share the view that they live as part of nature rather than contrary to it. Serenity exists among the people of Scandinavian countries just as it does among the Basques. The people of Norway's fjord country, for instance, seem at peace with their surroundings, despite the fact that the Norwegian terrain can be precipitous, the ground hard to plow, the weather destructive to crops. The mountain farmers of Norway's Stavanger region have invented new ways to clear away rocks and reclaim land from the ocean. This mountain country consists of 125,000 square miles, of which only four percent is arable. Unlike their American counterparts, ninety percent of Norway's farm families own less than twenty-five acres of land, but the Norwegians do not complain about these small plots.

Generalizations about mountain people are dangerous, of course, for exceptions are easily noted. Judgments must be narrowed to small regions or particular valleys.

133

*Snow-capped High Atlas
Mountains look down on fertile
valleys of Morocco. Home of Berbers
like tribesman above, Atlas
are rich in phosphates—and
racked by earthquakes.*

135

Traveling north through the British Isles makes one immediately aware of a strong regional identity. Mount Snowdon, at 3,600 feet (1,097 m) is, you are told emphatically, not in England but in Wales, and the villagers are not English but Welsh. On a bus heading north from Glasgow, a passenger inquires of his neighbor if he is English. "We're Scotch. Scots. Scotsmen," the man says with some indignation. The Scots are Highlanders. To them, the distinction is important and is delivered with a special pride. You are left with no doubt.

Highland people are quite an independent lot, especially with regard to the English. A hundred years ago, Wordsworth addressed a poem to a Highland girl: "Thou wear'st upon thy forehead clear the freedom of the mountaineer." This sense of independence characterizes the Scots sheepherder. He may live at the end of the manor valley, closed in by mountains. He avoids travel, and in winter he bides his time curing sheepskins. "When I lived there," writes Alastair Reid, the Scots poet, "we knew nothing of the rest of the world. Even today, the Scots are curiously disinterested in it. They live at their own remove."

In the Scots mountain country, the sun emerges only on rare occasions. Even ten to fifteen cloudless summer days are appreciated. Mountain paths remain drenched for weeks, and wet mists drift across the roofs. The generous hot Highland breakfasts are dictated by these days of rain and cold.

As I traveled north through the Highlands, I noticed that most of the people wore dour expressions on their pale faces. A citizen of Edinburgh told me, perhaps with a slight touch of malice, that the Scots get more surly as one continues north. This seemed to be true. By the time I reached Fort William, the town under Ben Nevis, the locals seemed downright mournful. What stern features!

But once a year even sober Fort William comes to life with a public event that sheds some light on the Highland Scot's nature. The occasion is the Ben Nevis foot race, which pits local lads against each other and against the vastness of Scotland's highest peak. Women are welcome to enter the race, too, but not many show up. Participants start from the outskirts of Fort William, climb to the top of the peak, and then race back down. They may choose any route they wish. Some slosh through waters, slide down grassy knolls on their backsides, dart down steep pebbly trails, and leap like chamois from rock to rock. I saw several contestants take dramatic falls that cut their knees severely. Medical help? Aye, but later. Not now. Persevering mountain men! First they must finish the race.

What about the mountain women? Almost without exception everywhere in the mountain world, the women work as hard as their men, sometimes harder. The Scotswoman is famous in that respect, but she is far better off than her sisters in South America or in the Himalayas, where the work is more grueling and the food less plentiful. The Indian or mestiza woman of the Andes ages quickly. Too much childbearing leaves its mark. At the biological age of forty, a Nepalese woman may look as if she is sixty. When she is not pregnant, a Sherpani is expected to carry loads equal to those carried by her husband.

Hard work? One need only go to the Swiss Alps for a look at the farm wives of the Bernese Oberland or of the Appenzell region. Swiss dairywomen keep busy from dawn to dusk. They cook, mend, scrub, churn, clean, sew, spin, harvest—and then tend to their men. For centuries, the high Alpine ramparts of Switzerland kept out influences that might weaken the traditional patriarchy. According to Swiss law, a wife was forbidden to take a job outside the home or even to have money of her own without her husband's permission. It was not until the 1970s that Swiss women were permitted to vote or to hold elective offices. For people who live behind the earth's crests and cornices, customs change slowly.

The civilized, disciplined Swiss, hemmed in by sheer geography for most of the year, have always been conservative. Wasn't Switzerland among the first nations to keep out the streams of refugees that might upset their orderly, industrious land? Generations of Swiss peasants spent their entire lives on a single piece of topography. Consider the *senner*—the dairyman and cheesemaker. In May or June each year, many of these men leave their families to drive their cattle onto the highest grassy slopes, the so-called *alm*. Here, many kilometers from other people, a man occupies a simple cabin, spending most of the summer with only cattle for company. For several months, he sees no other humans, reads no newspapers, and hears no radio. He milks his cows and listens to the tinkle of their bells. He plays midwife and doctor to his cattle, makes cheese, mends fences, chops wood, fixes the roof. And he watches the familiar old mountains. A summer spent in this manner can change a man in many ways. Some of these loners actually forget how to communicate with human beings. Living among animals creates taciturn men.

But the twentieth century has abbreviated the solitude for many of these men. Now they may occasionally interrupt their retreat to take some of their products to a dairy cooperative in the valley. Often they see hikers on the summits and may even put them up in their haylofts. Occasionally their sons visit and help to milk the cows. Their wives may come to their cabins to visit, or they may go home to spend a night or two. In many Alpine areas, there is a midsummer festival, with beer drinking, Alphorn blowing, wrestling competitions, and ram fights. Then comes another stay on the mountain.

In the fall, the dairymen descend into the valley with their cattle and the newborn calves. Often the biggest cow in the herd is decorated with mountain flowers for the occasion. Each man's wagon is loaded with cheeses weighing twenty to thirty pounds apiece. On the alm, the dairyman cannot be in touch with his times. Such mountain folk do not venture far. Some Swiss—the oldsters of

137

*Cuillin Hills of the Inner Hebrides
isle of Skye rise only to some
3,000 ft (914 m), but rugged slopes and
sheer precipices leave little
arable land for Scottish crofter.*

Andermatt, for example—have never traveled abroad, and perhaps only once in their entire life have they been as far as Zurich, a distance of about fifty miles. Like some Scots Highlanders who speak dialects that cannot be understood in the next valley, the people in Switzerland's isolated *kantone* (provinces) speak a language that is unintelligible to the rest of the Swiss population.

Paralleling the Scots, too, the Swiss rank as top virtues precision, neatness, hard work, and thrift. "If a Swiss eats a nail, a screw will come out," say the Germans. The mountain dwellers themselves are loath to speak about their core philosophy, but anecdotes reveal much about the character of these prudent people. In the beginning, so a tale told to me in Austria's Arlberg goes, God allowed the Swiss to make three wishes. Immediately they ordered the biggest mountains, and for their second wish, they asked for a cow that gave milk. The grateful Swiss then offered a small tumbler of milk to their benefactor.

"That was fine milk, thank you," God said. "Now what is your third wish?"

"Two francs and forty centimes, please," the Swiss said.

Mountain people should not be judged too severely for this attitude. Wherever they live in the mountain world, they are practically born knowing they must grab at every chance to secure themselves. The next blizzrd —or perhaps a lack of snow—might mean a poor season. For many mountain dwellers, the horizon ends at the nearest mountain pass, and this is enough of a barrier to cast doubt even on the fellow in the next valley. Flatlanders are cetainly suspect. Sir Arnold Lunn liked to tell about an Alpine ski race in which the referee could not be a foreigner, an understandable rule for a mountain community. But the villagers went a step further and voted against a "foreigner" from Bern, the country's capital, because it happens to be in flat country. Citizens living in Zermatt, a village at the base of the mighty Matterhorn, the imposing 14,698-foot (4,480-m) giant of the Alps, distrust those who live in the Rhône valley, only fifty miles away. People of Grindelwald still feel superior to the descendants of eighteenth-century "immigrants" from the Swiss lake country. Conceit? Perhaps. But mostly it is a fierce and intractable independence that, in varying degrees, is bred into people of the mountains everywhere.

Mountain people treasure their peace and freedom so greatly that they may fight to preserve it. The Tyroleans of western Austria have enjoyed many centuries of freedom. They were never serfs, and when they don regional costumes, they favor a regal red, in contrast to the gray Loden fabric worn by peasants of other regions. Citizens of Innsbruck, the Tyrol capital and winter sports center, were not happy with the Nazi regime during World War II. Some became resistance fighters; others went abroad to escape Nazi domination. When Hitler turned the region over to Mussolini, the local populace refused to bow to the Italians. They smuggled arms across

the Alps and shot at the occupiers, fighting to retain their independence. The lighthearted flatland Viennese could not understand the heroic stance of their Alpine compatriots.

Mountain people are often deeply religious. The supernatural provides comfort at great heights, where it is easy to feel set apart from ordinary forces. Throughout Europe, the mountains are dotted with places of worship: in Spain there is Montserrat, northwest of Barcelona, presumed site of the Castle of the Holy Grail; Mount Subasio, in Italy's Apennines, offers a hospitable slope to St. Francis' church at Assisi; the tiny Romanesque church of St. Michel d'Aiguille perches on the needle rock at Le Puy, in the old lace-making region of south-central France; the devotional city of Oberammergau rests below the Zugspitze in the Bavarian Alps.

Whether Austrians, Italians, Swiss, or Germans, the inhabitants of Alpine villages were greatly influenced by Christianity. The first missionaries arrived early in the post-Christian era and left their mark. Every mountain hamlet has its church. In rural Austria, more than eighty percent of the population is Catholic. Churches gave the villages cohesion, the priests and pastors attending births, deaths, and weddings. Even today the church bells in some villages toll at 6:00 A.M., at noon, and again at 7:00 P.M., echoing through the mountains.

139

But some customs predate the Christian era, going back to heathen times. Faced with hardships year after year, these early mountain people understandably took whatever precautions they thought might make their life easier, and some of their superstitions persist today as traditions. In the Tyrol, for instance, the coming of spring is announced by young boys who crack whips as they run through village streets. The lashings supposedly drive winter away. In Switzerland I saw processions of villagers banging drums and ringing bells for the same reason. In some of these performances, the participants wear ferocious masks, originally meant to drive away evil spirits and to conceal the mummer's identity, thus preventing the thwarted spirit from taking revenge.

But times are changing. In many areas in the past, a person would live his entire life in the house of his birth—a house that has already served the family clan for hundreds of years. Newer Alpine generations receive more education and may travel more. They are more sophisticated than their elders.

But throughout the mountain world, an unexplainable loyalty to the mountains remains untouched. Carinthians, for example, have seen their peaks thousands of times, but they never stop talking about them. I know natives of places like Aspen, Zermatt, and Innsbruck who cling to their high country forever. Living anywhere else in the world would be unthinkable.

La Paz, Bolivia; Chalt, Pakistan; Lhasa, Tibet; Santorini, Greece; Zer-

matt, Switzerland—mountain communities all, yet as diverse as their surrounding massifs. Variety in the mountain world is not limited only to the shapes of the ranges, the geology of the lands, or the climate and moods of the local people, but extends as well to the settlements and resorts. They may differ in looks from one ridge to the next. Location, size, age—all have a bearing.

I have seen Italian towns hanging from the hills like grapes from arbors and others stacked like dice on mountain shelves. In the Spanish Pyrenees, the villagers' rock-built abodes look like the jagged mountains that provided their stone. Spanish inns, or *pousadas*, and the modest farms—they recall their origins. The characteristics of Alpine towns vary even from border to border. There is Chiasso in the Italian Alps, with its nude, craggy stone houses, and just a few hours away there is Lech, Austria, where the stucco buildings are creamy white.

How does a mountain community acquire its special appearance, its individuality? One must look to the particular country, as well as to the area's history, terrain, climate, and income. Is it a new village? Did it have time for growth? If so, how much time? Five years? Five centuries? Does the community attract the right number of people, or too many? Is it isolated? Has it been by-passed?

If a community stands on a plateau or in a high valley, like some of the population centers in the Russian Urals, strongly built drab barracks may house the people. But what about the villages that hug high mountainsides? Mountains create a construction situation entirely different from the plains. "The load requirements must be met," one builder told me. "Fire is a constant threat. Water sources may be hard to reach. Heat loss is critical, and wind must be taken into account." Wind, in particular, explains why so many mountain villages —especially in the Andes, Alps, and Himalayas —look so compact. The dwellings are grouped close together as a shield against the wind. Compared with lowland houses, those of the mountains have thicker walls to keep out the cold, and the roofs are stronger or more deeply slanted to withstand the snow. To be sure,

141

Italian hill towns, like
Montefegatesi (above) have
huddled for safety
since Middle Ages. Left:
Mountain people, such
as South Tyrol wood carver
(l), often are deft
artisans. Even in summer,
Swiss village (top r)
appears braced for deep
snow. Broad dairylands of
Inn River valley (below).

143

there are regional variations, depending on the climate, availability of materials, and the mountain people's economic levels.

Many houses along the lower slopes of Afghanistan's Hindu Kush range are three-storied and have elaborately carved doors. The size of the house and the character of its decorations are marks of the owner's wealth. In Nepal, at 5,000 feet and higher, most of the houses are stone or mud-brick, and they too are three-storied. The lower floor is for livestock, tools, and the family dog. A slanted notched log usually serves as the stairway to the second-floor living area, and the third floor is an open roofed area used for storage. On the second floor is a large stove or fireplace used both for heating the house and for cooking. This stove is the center of life for these mountain people. Here the women tend to their children and cook the family's meals of vegetables, rice, and occasionally yak meat. Near this source of heat are the rugs or bamboo mats on which the family sleeps. Along the walls are shelves holding utensils and crocks of rice and grain. The windows are small and covered with paper, and there are no chimneys, so the air is usually full of smoke. But in this room the proud and cheery people drink their *chang* (beer), gossip, and entertain friends. The houses have only one door, and it is seldom closed. "People walk in and out all day," writes one trekker, "and every arrival is cause for a minor celebration."

Mountain people shape their community over generations, influencing both its appearance and its moods. As a driver nears Taos, New Mexico, he has no doubt that this is a mountain town. From the southwestern plains the road curves and rolls uphill through sage country, then into deep forests on the slopes. The leaves scintillate, framing the flanks of the mountains. Rivers tumble from the Sangre de Cristo Mountains, and the road skirts rushing water. Then, at nearly 7,000 feet (2,134 m), there is Taos. It soothes the eyes. The mountain town is all earth-colored New Mexican adobe. With a population of 2,500, Taos remains an endearing spot—somnolent, sensual, still strongly influenced by the Indians. They make turquoise jewelry, fashioning it by hand and doing remarkable things with silver. Because of the area's great beauty, Taos has attracted generations of artists, and Taos art galleries sell paintings that depict the gentle, swirling scenery surrounding the adobe houses. Summers here are warm, but late fall and winter have an edge to them.

In some places, a village may change before the people's eyes. Indifference makes fertile soil for greed. First come the real-estate speculators and quick-profit artists. Not far behind are the cheap builders. But sometimes enough townspeople awaken in time to prevent damage. Santa Fe, the capital of New Mexico, is a mountain town—at 7,000 feet, the highest city in the United States—that has fought valiantly and successfully to keep expansion down and preservation and restoration up. It remains untouchable. Builders must observe strict rules: no plastic, no flickering lights, no obnoxious signs, and a strict limit on the height of new buildings. *Muy bien!*

Woodstock, Vermont, is one of several New England communities that have preserved their charm. Set in the Green Mountains, lush green in summer and red in autumn, Woodstock has insisted on maintaining its lovely eighteenth-century houses with their tidy dormers and sparkling exteriors. Even in the mountain community of Stowe, Vermont, much bigger and more commercial than Woodstock, the heart of New England still beats. It has been on the map since 1794, and some of its snug white houses, red barns, and spires have changed as little as the Vermont winters. The conservative, independent, and tradition-bound inhabitants of Stowe, Woodstock, and similar places have not forgotten that "Vermont" is French for "green mountain." They chill at the notion of tree choppers and tractor drivers carving up the scenery.

The same sentiments prevail in some Austrian mountain hamlets. The old villages in the Arlberg region distrust the flashily new. Lech dates to the thirteenth century. In its church are the records of all baptisms since 1433, of local marriages since the 1500s. The village is ensconced in a tight valley and is topped by a fairy-tale land of open meadows, most handsome and photogenic under snow cover. There are no trains or planes to Lech, Oberlech, or Zuers, which is the valley's last and highest village before one encounters the Flexen Pass. A bus runs to St. Anton, and a properly equipped automobile can get through —unless an avalanche halts the traffic, as it does at least once every winter.

Whatever its age, location, or architecture, and whether simple or elaborate, contemporary or futuristic, the sudden sight of a little mountain community is comforting to the traveler. A roof overhead, food and drink, and a bed for the night. The feelings of gratitude and security have been universally shared by all who have sojourned in the mountain world, no matter when or where or by what means, on foot, skis, or wheels. It is easy to imagine the medieval traveler's sigh of relief upon reaching the inn of an Italian hill town or at finding shelter from a snowstorm in an Alpine village. Or think back to the frontier days of western America. A stagecoach crawls up switchbacks of dusty roads, with too many hours between stops, fatiguing men and horses alike. Then a few modest clapboard buildings come into view. Soon there is freshly baked bread and steaming soup on a rough-hewn table. A night's sleep in a room smaller than a monk's cell, but out of the summit winds.

It still happens today. A cluster of houses at 14,000 feet is a welcome sight to the modern trekker in the Himalayas. Or a Yankee motorist crossing South America with an ailing station wagon hopes he will soon get to a city— and there, at nearly 12,000 feet, is La Paz, Bolivia. Gasoline and water, food and wine! Maybe he will find the right mechanic in Quito, Ecuador (9,350 ft/2,850 m), or in Bogota, Colombia (8,700 ft/2,652 m).

Miracles in the mountains!

145

6

Mountain versus Man

*Preceding pages: Expedition climbing
Mount McKinley for first time
by new Traleika Spur route in 1972
encounters avalanching snow.
Above: Guards ascend Schiahorn
above the Parsenn, the Swiss
ski resort, to trigger avalanches
"by hand" as ski safety measure.*

A mountain can be a formidable adversary, not just to the climber who dares its heights, but to the errant soldier, the pilgrim, the merchant-trader venturing through its passes, to the indigenous herdsman in search of grass for his flocks, and to the engineer who undertakes to blast and bend it to his purposes. All may have cause to regret their rashness.

Although its mass and density appear unyielding, a mountain is constantly in motion—heaving and thrusting in the process of new creation, or deteriorating under the inexorable forces of erosion. Water in all its forms—as snow, glacial ice, rain, frost, dew—abrades the mountain surfaces and, seeping through fissures, hollows caverns and passageways internally, as well. The endlessly patient wind picks at the softer constituents of conglomerate rock, reducing it by a grain of sand, of talc, of limestone, until, inevitably, it crumbles. Temperature induces structural failure by alternations of hot expansion and cold contraction. And storms by their violence speed the process of destruction.

Yet the hazards of the mountain environment have seldom deterred man from entering it and wreaking his will upon it. Bold hunters roamed the Alps ten thousand years ago, Celtic tribesmen traversed the chain long before the birth of Christ.

Perhaps the most notable assault on the Alps came during the Second Punic War, in 218 B.C. Carthage, having lost most of its fleet in sea battles with Rome, could no longer contest control of the Mediterranean.

Hannibal, the cunning and resolute Carthaginian general, decided to march an army overland, cross the Alps, and fall on the Roman rear. It was an audacious scheme and a fantastic logistical exercise. He had forty thousand troops, nine thousand horses, nine elephants, and a full baggage train.

Starting from Spain, he crossed the Pyrenees and the Rhône river before the Romans could intercept him. He moved up the Rhône valley and entered the Alpine passes, just which ones Polybius, the Greek historian who is the principal chronicler of this enterprise, does not say. Perhaps they bore no names in those days. The best guesses are that he used either the Little St. Bernard, which connects French Savoie with Italian Val d'Aosta, or Mont Genèvre.

It appears that Hannibal underestimated the mountains. He evidently got lost in the Alpine heights. Men and horses tumbled off the high paths and fell into crevasses. Mountain folk, resenting the alien intrusion, rolled boulders onto the heads of Hannibal's archers and infantrymen. Often the army was halted by snow masses or steep rock headwalls. Polybius says Hannibal cleverly used vinegar to "dynamite" rocks blocking passage. The acid was poured into cracks in the rocks, then fire heated the rocks and boiled the vinegar, which expanded explosively. It is not clear how much vinegar the general carried in the pack train to accomplish all this blasting, but it is true that boiling vinegar will generate explosive gases, particularly if used with limestone.

149

The crossing took fifteen days, the entire march five months, and the army was depleted by casualties by the time it finally descended onto the plains of Lombardy. But with the initiative in his hands, Hannibal gave the Romans several sound thrashings over the next several years, until his position at the end of an attenuated supply line made it impossible to reinforce him sufficiently to take Rome.

In centuries to come the Romans paved some of the roads into the Alps, and eventually there was enough traffic to warrant building shelters in some of the passes. One of the best-known hospices topped the Great St. Bernard, and at great sacrifice a number of smaller churches and chapels arose.

But basic fears of the mountains were slow to be assuaged. For centuries, Mont Blanc was known as "the accursed." Peasants peopled the mountains with a variety of supernatural beings: elves and dwarfs, sprites, ondines, and magical beasts. During the Middle Ages "flying dragons" were seen in the Alps; as late as 1726 scientists were still writing about them. Engravings of the period show white, fire-breathing worms slithering down white glaciers.

Peasant apprehension was not unreasonable. Mountains have always been a hazard for trespassers, and even a threat to villagers living on the slopes or in the valleys. Hunters were known to fall into crevasses, disappearing completely until another season or another year, when the creeping glacier delivered a body, frozen and intact, from its constantly moving leading edge.

Human beings learned not only to fear ice and avalanche, but volcanic fire, as well. Lava from active volcanoes has buried villages everywhere in the world—most recently in Iceland—and set forests aflame.

Mountains were the greatest barrier to exploration and settlement of the North American continent. Most of the affection for high mountain country has come only in recent times, for apart from a few adventuresome priests, botanists, and hunters or trappers, the masses stayed in the valleys. Spanish conquistadors and their padres, for instance, were unprepared for the snow and winds at 10,000 to 14,000 feet in the Rockies, but in the years that followed, many brave emigrants made their way over the mountains on the way west. An Indian warned John Charles Frémont that he would find nothing in the High Sierra but "rock upon rock, snow upon snow." The Indians had already trodden countless trails, and these were followed by mountain men like Kit Carson and Jim Bridger, and by surveyors searching out solid knowledge of the mountains and their high passes in order to plot the best routes for transcontinental railroads. Some travelers were treated benignly; others suffered great hardships or experienced tragedy.

No party endured more misfortune than that of Jacob and George Donner, who were joined by several other families, eighty-six people in all, on a journey across the High Sierra. They began their trek westward from Springfield, Illinois, in 1845. No one in

150

their party had experience in the high country. Worse, the Donners ignored the advice of local mountain men and chose their own ill-fated route. By the time they reached Utah, some of the wagons had already fallen apart, and sickness assailed the party. But the Donners elected to continue. The Rockies delayed them, upsetting their timetable, and it was November when they finally reached the High Sierra. Now they were beset by the perils of a harsh mountain winter as sudden snows blanketed the slopes. The party was trapped. Food supplies ran out. The Donner Pass nightmare—one of exhaustion, freezing, great hunger, and even cannibalism—lasted for thirty-three days. Only about half of those who had started the trip survived to continue to California.

High mountains have always been formidable adversaries for road builders. Construction of a sixteen-mile road across Switzerland's St. Gotthard Pass, for instance, required ten years to complete—from 1820 to 1830. Even today, many roads in the Alps are closed from October until June. Highway builders always anticipate more problems in the mountains. The unexpected seems to be the rule, with the great variations in soil, rocks, and gradient now demanding a curve or a serpentine course, then requiring a straight road that mounts and dips toward more loops. Any time of year the mountains may show their teeth unexpectedly. High above timberline, the warm summer sun may melt glacial ice and unleash a rock slide that blocks the roadway or sends trucks and heavy equipment tumbling down the slopes.

Rich finds of gold and silver spurred the construction of toll roads in the U.S. West, but in some instances, the steep terrain and the need for switchback curves swallowed a company's funds. The twelve-mile road from Ouray to Red Mountain, Colorado, for instance, had to be cut through solid rock. Another famous pay-as-you-go road serpentined for forty-five miles across stormy 11,000-foot (3,352-m) Berthoud Pass, its terminus at Hot Sulphur Springs.

Toll roads proved to be a bonanza in the Colorado Rockies, its deep gorges and forested canyons leading up to large bare areas above the timberline. For about five dollars, an entrepreneur could secure a road-toll charter from the legislature. He built a road up the slope, and the rest was easy: a toll station, often coupled with a bridge or a wooden gate and a fenced hillside, was placed in the narrow canyon, forcing the traveler to stop and pay. Tolls were based on mileage and on the customer. The fare for a one-span team and a wagon was perhaps a dollar for a short stretch. A horseman paid twenty-five cents, goats and sheep were assessed at a nickel apiece. Indians and funeral processions often rode through free.

Some mountains were so smooth they caused builders no trouble at all. A few wagon trips over the crests, a few stone markers, and some newspaper ads announcing the new toll road was all they needed to be in business. Selling whisky, beer, and food at toll

153

Preceding pages: In laborious slow motion, Mendenhall Glacier of southeastern Alaska extrudes an ice mass which crashes heavily into the sea. This kind of breakaway formation of icebergs is also called "calving."

Disaster Areas: Highway at Rocky Gap, Virginia (r) is blocked by 150,000 cubic feet of landslide. Boulders (below) are part of ice wall that thundered down slope of Huascarán in 1962, devastating six Peruvian villages and burying 3,000 people.

houses increased the owners' profits. Later the toll houses became stagecoach stops. The longest of these pay-as-you-travel highways led from Placerville, California, to Virginia City, Nevada—a 101-mile trip, mostly across the High Sierra. During the 1860s and the heyday of the Comstock mines, this toll road netted its owners about $640,000 a year. The route was studded with hotels, saloons, and even general merchandise stores. Stages used it, and so did the express lines that transported gold. Such roads developed plenty of mail traffic, too, along with armies of loaded donkeys, hunters on horseback, and thousands of miners seeking their fortunes in the mountains. All through the 1860s and 1870s, in fact, business was brisk as thousands streamed across the Continental Divide.

The nineteenth century was marked by great engineering exploits in the mountains of the United States and Europe as part of the drive for railroad transportation. In America the dream of a transcontinental line to link the Atlantic and Pacific coasts spurred efforts to survey possible routes as early as the 1850s, despite the ranges that barred the way. Major-General Grenville M. Dodge explored a westward route for the Union Pacific, and Theodore M. Judah found an eastward path through the Sierra Nevada for the Central Pacific. Shortly after the Civil War ended, the first rails were laid.

It had been hoped that the U.P. could pass through Denver, but Dodge found a more feasible route through the Rockies farther north, beyond Cheyenne. Nonetheless, as the construction gangs left the Great Plains, some five hundred miles beyond their starting point at Omaha, and ascended into the mountains, they soon found themselves working at altitudes of 8,235 feet (2,510 m). Thereafter, they had 150 miles of "mountain work," areas difficult enough to warrant government subsidies of $48,000 per mile, as opposed to $16,000 on the plains and $32,000 in moderately complex country.

The Rockies were surmounted in 1867–68, the route through the Wasatch Mountains of Utah was graded in the winter of 1868. Dodge always said that his surveyors had studied the mountains en route to find slopes least exposed to heavy snows and landslides, and, indeed, when much of the original work was redone in later years to replace iron rails with steel, to adjust grades and curves and widen cuts, the U.P. engineers found there was little they could do to improve either on Dodge's route or his construction. Over more than one thousand miles of railway through several mountain ranges he had nowhere exceeded a gradient of ninety feet in a mile, although up to 116 was permissible.

Perhaps the most difficult period had been the winter of '68, when grading was being done over the Wasatch. The ground was frozen so hard that it had to be blasted like rock. Track was laid in the dead of winter, atop snow and ice, and Dodge saw one train, loaded with construction materials, slide helplessly over an embankment and into a ditch.

156

Two Devil's Bridges (Teufelsbrücke)
—a serpentine old one and a straight and narrow
new—cut through the Alpine jumble of
central Switzerland like a pictorial riddle
by Dutch artist M. C. Escher.

The Central Pacific, thrusting eastward, covered fewer but dramatically more difficult miles. Starting from Sacramento, the C.P.'s crews—Chinese, eventually numbering some ten thousand, as opposed to the U.P.'s Irishmen—were almost immediately into the Sierra Nevada mountains. Grading meant, alternately, blasting cuts and filling ravines. It was hoped, of course, that the debris from the cuts could be used in the ravines, and occasionally it could. But, because of the toughness of the rock, such large charges of blasting powder had to be used that often the explosions simply blew everything to bits. Whereupon thousands of tons of fill for the next gorge had to be hauled by horsecart along the right of way.

Whole peaks had to be physically altered to accommodate the roadbed. Slopes had to be terraced, shelves carved out of the solid rock. And except for the blasting powder (dynamite was invented in 1866 but never used on the C.P.), all work was done by hand, with picks, shovels, crowbars, sledges.

Everything had to be hauled into the mountains—rails, spikes, fish plates, and ties, although lumber was readily available from the forests of California and Nevada. At one point, thirty sawmills were operating simultaneously just to produce railroad ties. Elements were carried forward on flatcars, and the line was advanced by an orderly procedure. Twenty pairs of tie men placed a tie every fourteen feet. (In California they used redwood!) Fillers followed, filling in spaces with crossties. Iron men, four per rail (it weighed some fifty pounds per yard), laid the track, followed by four gaugers to make sure the rails were precisely four feet eight and a half inches apart. Head spikers drove six spikes per rail. Back spikers and screwers put in the remaining four spikes per rail and bolted on the fish plates.

(Dodge calculated that at three blows per spike, ten spikes per rail, four hundred rails to a mile, and eighteen hundred miles from Omaha to San Francisco, the sledge hammers were swung 21 million times!)

Finally came the chain gang, backfillers to tamp earth between the ties, and track liners with crowbars to make final adjustments in alignment and level.

The Central Pacific seems to have had the worst of it, winter-wise. The winter of 1864–65 was mild, but as luck would have it, the railroad ran out of money and no work could be done. By the time more capital was raised, the winters had turned savage. In 1865–66 the area was covered with five feet of snow by December 1, enough to stop work on tunnels, and below the snow line to turn the roads to impassable quagmires. In 1866–67, there were forty-four storms, ranging from squalls to two-week gales that brought up to ten feet of snow. Because of the moderate Pacific climate, however, the snow was damp and heavy. Rain, melting snow, and storms generally were severe enough to knock out trestles and wash away embankments.

Tunnels—there were eleven of them in twenty-seven miles at the Sierra summit—could be worked on during bad weather,

159

but many of them required timber lining, and often both entrances and exits were blocked by snow or landslides. A bucker plow—a wedge fastened on the front of a car loaded with pig iron and pushed by three locomotives—fought the cascading earth and drifting snows, literally taking a run and bucking its way through the debris—and derailing itself when the resistance was too great.

In many areas there was nothing for it but to build snowsheds and galleries to keep the track clear. By 1869 there were thirty-seven miles of them.

By fall of 1867 the last of the summit tunnels was completed and the crews, which had now completed some fifty miles of track at above 5,000 feet (1,524 m) elevation, began to work downhill toward Truckee. But winter came, and with it a total of forty feet of snow. At times, it was eighteen feet deep on the level.

Thereafter, the route eased for the C.P., and on May 10, 1869, the two roads met at Promontory Point, in the high country of Utah. The final spike was driven, the nation was joined.

This story is perhaps the favorite, because of the dramatic competition and because it was a first, but many of the railroads which followed, adding strands to the connecting cross-country link, had their battles with the mountains, too. Jim Hill performed prodigies with his Great Northern, which pierced the Rockies near Great Falls, Montana, and overcame tremendous obstacles to reach Seattle

some six years later. The Northern Pacific and Canadian Pacific also had spectacular difficulties, the former with the Cascades, the latter with the Canadian Rockies.

Tunnel builders met similar problems in the mountains. In some places, the mountains offer no good way of getting over them, and so there is no choice but to burrow through. Experts say that tunneling techniques lag behind those of other engineering endeavors, but the job is much more difficult. Tunnels are unpredictable and expensive ventures. A mountain may offer sufficient resistance to double or even triple careful estimates of the man hours needed for drilling, blasting, rock hauling, buttressing, timbering, and the many other labors involved in completing a tunnel for use by trains and cars. In 1857, Europe's most skillful engineers could not foresee that it would take fourteen years to build the thirteen-mile Fréjus, the first long tunnel through the Alps. It took eight years of drilling to finish the nine-mile Swiss St. Gotthard railroad tunnel. The contractor, who supervised the job himself and stood for days in the icy water that poured down the walls, suffered so many frustrations that he died of heart failure in his tunnel.

In 1969, contractors began to build a second tunnel through the St. Gotthard Pass. The massif fought the intruders from the start, and they encountered situations so complex that they advanced only about two miles per year. When geologists and engineers made their first test drills, the instruments they used to calculate approximate stresses were so sensi-

*Mountains are low and tracks level along this
stretch of the Southern Pacific (l), but multiple
diesels imply tougher gradients elsewhere. Above: Union
Pacific, engineering line change in Wyoming,
found best route through the Rockies in 1860s.*

163

tive they were able to monitor the mountain's movements in tiny fractions of inches. Still, with long tunneling experience behind them, the Swiss knew that these pilot bores would probably not duplicate the actual tunnel, for the pattern of rock layers in the much-folded and twisted Alps is wholly unpredictable. Engineering reports later revealed that much of the anticipated hard granite turned out to be crystalline, crumbling easily. As the drill crews advanced through the early 1970s, the Gotthard massif bulged its muscles. "The mountain exerts pressure from every direction, trying to squeeze shut the tunnel portals," one report explained. Progress was possible only by holding up tunnel ceilings and walls with massive concrete buttresses, steel arches, wood beams, and other supports.

Sometimes a thick fog would slow down work inside the tunnel. At other times it was tropically hot in the shafts. During the first five years, the crew changed five times. Such a labor turnover is unusual in Europe. The St. Gotthard automobile tunnel still has not been completed. It is not expected to be open until 1985 or perhaps even later. The mountain has made a mockery of famed Swiss punctuality.

A tunnel unquestionably saves time for a motorist, and it relieves him of having to cross tortuous mountain passes. For example, it takes only about fifteen minutes to drive the 7.2 miles through Mont Blanc, Europe's highest mountain. The tunnel saves at least five hours of driving, and both the approach and exit views of the Alps are memorable. But high peaks are never tamed cheaply. The driver easily forgets that the tunnel cost six years of toil and $64 million. The Mont Blanc Tunnel proved a savage opponent when a sudden stream of trapped ice water propelled a metal bar through the body of a miner. Three other workers were killed in their camp by an avalanche. Falling rock masses buried equipment.

Tunnel builders in the United States faced similar surprises and delays. The Hoosac Tunnel in Massachusetts, the first American railroad tunnel through a mountain, must have set an all-time record, requiring twenty-one years (1852–73) to chew through a short five-mile stretch of the Green Mountains. In the process, it claimed nearly two hundred lives. Railroad tunnels in Washington's Cascade Mountains, short vehicular tunnels under the Alleghenies—all have cost more than anticipated.

Rock slides are commonplace in many parts of the mountain world. The first rays of the morning sun often trigger a cascade of rocks. It starts with a single boulder that falls faster and faster, crashing against the mountainside and dislodging other debris that goes with it into the abyss. Heavy rains may transform steep gulleys into chutes for a veritable bombardment of thundering stones. In the Crownet Pass section of British Columbia, tourists still inspect the giant scar caused by such a slide when an entire ridge suddenly broke off and dropped into the valley. One day in 1903, a crescent of Turtle Mountain in Alberta crashed down the mountainside. It took only ninety seconds for 90 million tons to cover part of a town and snuff out seventy lives. Volcanoes can also discharge rock masses from their rims or seams. In 1963, for example, one of Mount Rainier's 11,117-foot (3,388-m) satellites fell apart, and some 14 million cubic yards of debris rumbled down the slopes.

Villagers in the Alps call it the White Power and know that it can wipe out a village, a farmhouse, or an imprudent person. Always the Swiss have respected the mountain forces. In winter, the older, experienced skiers take no chances. During the 1960s, a Swiss magazine ran an article about an American ski racer who allegedly like to outrace small snow slides. The magazine claimed that the famous American enjoyed the sensation of snow pulsating at his heels. Avalanches challenged him to ski all the faster. A reporter's exaggeration? Or did this daring American actually like to antagonize high mountains? If so, the racer played a form of Russian roulette. One April day in 1964, the Swiss Institute of Snow Research and a local patrolman warned skiers of dangerous conditions. Several cold days followed by a sudden thaw had increased the possibility of avalanches, and the hazard was greatest at the higher altitudes. The bold American and a companion took a chance. Behind them came a 400-yard-wide, 600,000-ton monster. They tried to outski the avalanche, but it caught up with them. They courted White Death and lost.

To pit oneself against a giant mountain at a time when it might reply with a snow slide is purest folly. Yet I was guilty of such bravado once myself. Not too long ago, while a February blizzard raged, I headed straight into the teeth of avalanches on the Zugspitze, Germany's highest peak. Why did I seek out this thick-shouldered mountain? A sense of adventure? To mock death? Brinksmanship? A test of self in the face of great danger? Honestly, I do not know the answer.

My teen-age son had suggested that we take the tramway up to the Zugspitze's Osterfelderkopf, ski across to Hochalm and then down to Garmisch, the resort. Stephen did not know—and I never told him—that a few years earlier a powerful avalanche had swept down from the Zugspitze and snuffed out dozens of lives at the Schneefernerhaus Hotel. Some of the victims were hotel personnel, but most of them were tourist skiers. The sliding snow from the German peak caught many of them as they were relaxing in deck chairs on the hotel terrace.

We took the cable car straight to the top, a journey that nearly parallels the mountain's massive stone walls. I confess knowing that we were headed into potential danger. Perhaps I wanted to prove that I was unafraid. Stephen was innocent. We were on the afternoon's last tram.

"At your own risk," the operator told us. "There's no way back except on skis. Down unknown trails. Through the snowstorm." He tried to dissuade us. "*Lawinen*," he said darkly. "Avalanches."

165

Outracing avalanches is a hazardous, not to say foolhardy, enterprise in which skier's victory may be exhilarating, but his defeat permanent. Picture sequence shows how easily a loose-snow slide can be triggered, how quickly it moves on a steep slope.

*Mountain barriers to the transmission of
radio waves are overcome by line-of-sight towers
—some 25–30 miles apart—which serve as microwave relay
stations. This one, at 8,000 ft (2,438 m),
is on Oregon's Mount Hood.*

We joined him in the big square cabin. He shrugged, punched our tickets, and shut the door with finality. There were no other passengers. We were at the point of no return. Stephen compared the uphill ride with the astronaut's accelerating G-forces. It was a fair simile, for we were trapped in the capsule like spacemen in their rockets. Enormous gusts of wind shook the metal conveyance. The conductor held on tightly, stoically, accustomed to the Zugspitze's brutal moments. We clutched our sharp, upright skis as the capsule swayed over an abyss.

I felt strangely calm and safe when we reached the top, though the winds on the summit were ferocious. The conductor shouted that he had private sleeping quarters in the terminal where he himself would be staying overnight. We thanked him but shook our heads and began strapping on our skis while the tempest fired ice crystals into our faces. Stephen had studied the map, but now there were no landmarks—only walls of snow, blowing snow, stationary snow, descending snow. One of my gloves filled up with the white stuff, and I shook it out quickly. The remaining flakes melted. No need to add frostbite to our adventure.

Stephen broke trail, which is hard work—and especially so with an impatient father exhorting him to go faster because it would be dark in only half an hour. I kept thinking of the Schneefernerhaus avalanche. "No one could stay alive under those snows. As hard as reinforced concrete," rescuers later told the press.

We had to do at least ten miles on skis, and now we had no choice. Our route ran under steep slopes, the greatest avalanche dangers. As I poled along the hazardous trail, I wondered who had designed it. Then suddenly a ten-yard-long layer of white detached from above, and like a hundred emptied sacks of flour, rolled over Stephen's skis, burying him to his chest. He fell without an outcry. Broken leg? "Broken binding," he gasped. It was 5:00 P.M. on the forlorn, stormy Bavarian peak.

I could hear more slides now at a distance. Thoughts of death rolled through my mind. "Stay calm," I thought. "Don't panic." For a moment I listened to the mournful wind that drove dry, soft curtains into my face. My son stood without moving. The wind had deposited snow on his wool cap, jeans, and parka; snow stuck to his cheeks, brows, and eyelids. He looked down at his skis. Fog drifted across the slopes above us, but the mountain angled like a ship's hull, allowing me to look down: white, smooth, hard, and sheer.

"You're good with your hands," I said to Stephen. "Can you fix the binding? Please try."

Stephen nodded and then began concentrating on the mechanism. At that instant I heard a thunderclap and a long hiss that could mean only one thing: avalanche! We both looked in the direction of the sound but could see nothing. Too much fog. But we felt the blast of air on our faces. Did the avalanche go down a mile away? Was it only one of many more to come? We were unharmed, not even pushed or tossed about. I debated whether to return to the lift station, but we had already gone too far.

Meanwhile, Stephen had figured out what was wrong with his binding. Luckily, it wasn't broken, and he soon had it functioning again. I moved into the lead, noting

169

*Mont Blanc Tunnel:
World's longest vehicular
tube (7.5 miles), it
took seven years to bore,
working from both the
French and Italian sides.
Opposite: In process
7,500 ft (2,286 m)
below peak. Left: Just
before final blast.
Below l: Entrance on
French side. Right:
Midpoint, opening day.
Tunnel cost 17 lives.*

by the color of the snow that the sun was dropping rapidly now. I wanted to be up front so that if we ran into another slide I would be the one to face it first. Why not? I have already lived for five decades; my son for less than two. Strangely, there was only fog and more fog. Otherwise the mountain seemed to have quieted down. At 6,000 feet, the sky cleared, the wind beat a retreat, and it turned cold. Would this hold back further avalanches? Occasionally the Zugspitze's ski trails forced us to climb, slowing our pace considerably. Then we began our descent into the near darkness. Two hours later a reassuring sight greeted us: the lights of Garmisch blinking up from the valley. We made it safely down the last thousand feet. We were alive. We had won against the mountain. We had twisted its "white tail" and had had the last laugh. But the adventure was a foolish one that might have ended differently.

The U.S. Forest Service distinguishes two principal types of avalanches. Loose-snow avalanches are those that gather over a small area and then grow as they descend. The loose-snow avalanche moves as a formless mass and has little internal cohesion. Slab avalanches, in contrast, are massive from the beginning. They start when a large snow area begins to slide all at once, and there is a well-defined fracture line where moving crystals break away from stable ones. In slab avalanches the snow crystals tend to stick together, and there may be angular blocks or chunks of snow in the slide. A slope's steepness is the triggering factor, of course. Avalanches may occur on slopes ranging from 25 to 60 degrees. Smooth, grassy slopes are more likely to slide than are areas with big rocks, trees, or heavy brush, which help to anchor the snow. Avalanches are more probable after at least six to eight inches of new snow have fallen, and the danger may last for several weeks. Winds or a rapid rise in temperature add to the chances of a slide.

A skier can test a slope for its potential to slide. If he jabs his ski pole into the surface and finds fluffy snow on top with gradually harder snow deeper down, conditions are probably stable. But if there is a hard layer just under the surface and then a lot of loose, soft snow deep down, a slide is possible.

Most deaths due to avalanches could have been prevented if a few common-sense rules had been followed. It is foolish, for instance, to venture into avalanche country without the proper equipment. One of the most tragic accidents of recent years happened on Mount Temple, an 11,600-foot (3,536-m) peak in the Canadian Rockies. On that sad day a group of young boys visiting the area tried to go up the snow bowl. They had no experience, no ropes, no guide. They wore track shoes, baseball shoes, or sneakers. An avalanche killed almost all of them.

Loud noises can set off a slide. Avalanches are commonly started by the needless firing of guns in mountain country. Even a loud yell can bring down a slide.

In some parts of the world, great masses of snow still boil across highways, covering automobiles and creating other havoc. In the western United States and in Canada, highway crews blast avalanches with 75-mm howitzers or rifles to set them loose before they roar over a roadway on their own and perhaps trap motorists. Alpine nations such as Switzerland and Austria long ago learned how to reduce damage by deflecting the snow masses with special rails, fences, guards, and concrete walls. Antiavalanche tunnels and special galleries or roofs protect automobiles and trains in the Alps.

Experienced mountaineers, skiers, and snowshoers detour around areas where there are broken or stunted trees that indicate previous avalanche activity. They avoid steep gulleys, crossing over slopes as high as possible and traveling along ridges. A longer route can be a lifesaver. Some people wisely trail red avalanche cords behind them. A bit of red showing may give a clue to a person's whereabouts if he is caught in a slide. A newer invention is an electronic transceiver which emits continuous beeps that can be picked up by rescuers.

What do you do if you are caught in a slide? Call out to other members of your party to let them know where you are. This will help them find you if you do get buried by the snow. Dump your poles, skis, ice ax, and rucksack if possible. Keep in motion. Fight! Kick! Do everything possible to keep your body on top of the snow. Try to reach one side of the stream. In smaller avalanches, this can save your life. Try to clear a breathing space, and use your hands to keep the snow out of your nose and mouth. People have survived for hours under the snow when they had created an air space with their hands or arms. If you are buried, try not to panic. You will only use up valuable oxygen. Self-control is essential if you are to survive. You may even be able to dig yourself out. If you hear rescuers above you, don't waste your strength with a lot of yelling. Be calm. Let them dig down to you.

Man's adventuresome spirit and derring-do make him vulnerable, but at high altitudes he is out of his element. My son noted in his diary that the Himalayas seemed to call down to him, "You don't belong up here! This is the land of the gods!" In the high mountains, a human being is indeed a frail creature. Some people adapt quickly to high altitudes; others require days or even weeks to get adjusted. Some people live and work at elevations greater than 14,000 feet, but not everyone can do it. Mountain climbers admit that they begin to get sluggish and that their efficiency slows when they climb above 20,000 feet. At 25,000 feet, their mental faculties are greatly impaired, and the simplest tasks become extraordinarily difficult. Lack of oxygen retards thought processes, and any activity may result in lung problems or even in total collapse. At this point a quick descent to lower elevations becomes essential. A mountain reminds us that we must breathe to live.

But for some, to live means taking on the mountain adversary again the next day—and this time to make the summit.

173

7

7

Flora and Fauna

Preceding pages: Dall sheep of Alaska and northwestern Canada, and mountain goats (above), are white-coated —exception to rule that most alpine animals are darker than same or related species living at lower altitudes. Dark hues absorb heat, block harmful rays.

176

In the early 1890s, C. Hart Merriam and fellow workers of the U.S. Department of Agriculture surveyed the plants growing from the foothills to the highest peaks in the White Mountains of the Sierra Nevada in California. They reported an interesting discovery: a distinct banding or zoning of life forms as they moved from the lowlands to the snow-clad summits. Temperature, declining an average of 2 degrees F for each five hundred feet of rise, appeared to be the determining factor in the change from one zone to another, and the pattern was so chartable that the same general life zones could be predicted with reasonable accuracy for comparable elevations on other mountains. Equally interesting, identical banding was identifiable in moving from the equator to the poles.

For a classic illustration, consider a high mountain set in a tropical forest at the equator. Above the tropical zone, still recognizable for more than half a mile up the slopes, would be a band of deserts and grasslands followed by a band of deciduous forests and then by coniferous forests. Still higher would be the tundra, or alpine region, topped off with perpetual snow and ice. Within each of these broad regions, of course, would be smaller subdivisions. But on such an equatorial mountain four miles high, the same life zones would be encountered as in traveling from that same tropical forest to the poles, a distance of more than six thousand miles. Different species of plants and animals might live in the comparable zones, but many would bear striking resemblances to each other in basic features because of their similar living conditions.

Where Merriam did his work, there is no tropical zone. Only a few places in the world exhibit all of these bands clearly on one mountain, in fact, but they do occur. On a trek from Katmandu, Nepal, up Mount Everest in the Himalayas, one does indeed go from the tropics to the arctic, from a domain of palms and fig trees through a land of oaks and other deciduous trees, then spruce and fir, finally reaching a near-barren tundra separating the timberline from the snowy peak. This trip reveals also how some plants respond to growing conditions at varied altitudes. Rhododendrons abound in Nepal—some two hundred species in all—and at this elevation they are handsome, spindly shrubs flanking the trails that lead up the mountain. Midway, in the zone with a temperate climate, the rhododendrons grow as trees, some to fifty or even sixty feet tall. Still higher, where the temperature has dropped sharply, the rhododendrons shrink to shrub size. But everywhere, with their deep-green leaves and blood-red or purple blossoms, they are, as one Australian scientist wrote, "An orgy of color! An enchanted garden!"

All mountains do have life-zone systems. This is indisputable. They differ in specific character only because of the geographic location of the mountains, their height, and particular local conditions. In contrast to the Himalayas, a climb up Mount Kilimanjaro near the equator in eastern Africa starts in a rain forest, followed by a bamboo forest, then giant mossy heather trees, and finally, at 10,000 feet,

177

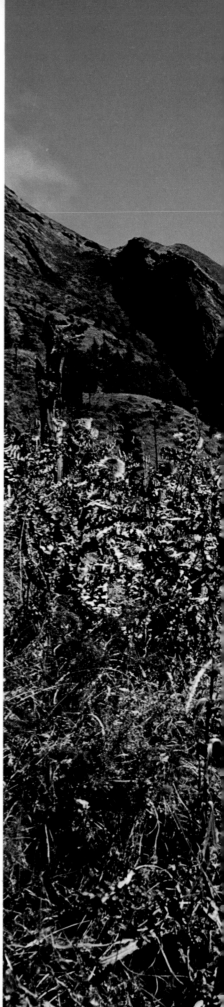

*Above: High Sierra pines,
California. Right:
Alpine zone of Ruwenzoris,
on Uganda-Zaire border.
Opposite: Flora
at 14,000 ft (4,267 m) on
south slope of
Dhaulagiri, Himalayas.*

178

a zone dominated by six-foot yuccalike African lobelias. Above these plants lie the tundra and then glacial snow and ice.

Merriam's life-zone concept received wide recognition, and biologists immediately began applying the principle broadly, classifying all plants and animals, whether mountain dwellers or not, according to the life zone in which they lived. Limitations soon became obvious. Merriam's zones were delineated strictly on the basis of temperature, constituting a biothermal approach to classifying plant and animal distribution. Geography and ecological factors made it difficult and in some cases impossible to apply the principle. Great variations, for example, do occur from one side of a mountain to the other—the north slope is definitely colder than the south, and the windward side wetter than the leeward. Because of latitude and other factors, the timberline is located at different elevations on mountains throughout the world. In the Himalayas, for example, trees may be found growing at about 14,500 feet (4,420 m), sometimes higher; on Mount Kilimanjaro at 14,000 feet (4,267 m). Moving farther north, timberline is at approximately 11,500 feet (3,505 m) in Colorado, 7,000 feet (2,134 m) in Montana's Glacier National Park, and 2,500 feet (762 m) in Alaska. The last of the trees is at about 6,000 feet (1,829 m) in the Bavarian Alps, 3,000 feet (914 m) in Norway's fjord country, and as low as 1,500 feet (457 m) in Wales and Scotland.

Though Merriam's life-zone system of classification has been largely aban-

doned as a useful ecological tool, the idea remains interesting. All plants and animals cannot be fit neatly into bands delineated by temperature, but a general understanding of the mountain world's flora and fauna based on the life-zone principle is certainly helpful.

At lower elevations in the mountain world, conditions for life are much like those of the surrounding land. Only rarely do they differ significantly, and so the slopes are invaded successfully by both plants and animals from the area. Some of the animals are transients, moving up the slopes in summer and returning to warmer lowlands in winter. Prime examples of this sort are deer and elk. Bears, too, roam over wide territories, though the mountains may be their escape from civilization. Many animals have been forced to move to the mountains for refuge, the high places becoming their last stronghold against encroaching circles of humanity. The American puma (also known as the cougar or mountain lion), most wide-ranging of all the cats, was not exclusively a mountain dweller originally, but the last of these big cats—now only a few thousand —survive principally in the remoteness of the mountains, individuals setting out on forays into the lowlands only when forced to by hunger. Those that have inhabited the mountains for generations display a characteristic typical of mountain animals—they are larger than those that have spent their lives in the lowlands. Males may measure more than eight feet long and weigh two hundred pounds, almost a third larger than the few cats of the same species still

*North American elk, or
wapiti (above), is a
transient, departing
heights in winter for warmer
lowlands. Giant panda
(l) of southern China is
an endangered species.
Llama (opposite),
a member of camel
family, thrives on high
plateaus of Andes.*

living in the Florida Everglades. Because of their larger size, mountain animals have proportionately less surface area in relation to body bulk and, as a result, they lose less body heat in the cold of the mountain world. The larger size also accommodates larger lungs and heart, adaptations necessary for warm-blooded animals in obtaining and utilizing sufficient oxygen in the rarefied atmosphere.

Another animal that turned long ago to the mountains is the giant panda. Though once widely distributed in eastern Asia, it has for centuries been limited to the bamboo forests of the Himalayas in southern China, where, at elevations of 5,000 to 10,000 feet, it feeds only on the shoots and tender branches of bamboo plants. But even in this retreat the giant panda's safety became so threatened that its survival is questionable, and the government of China has had to put the species under strict protection. Sharing portions of the bamboo forests with the giant panda are the smaller red panda and the golden or snub-nosed monkey, both bamboo eaters and both also endangered.

In Africa, the giant gorillas, largest of all the primates, inhabit principally the lowland equatorial forests, but one population long ago moved into the high forests on the volcanic mountains of Zaire, where they live at elevations of about 13,000 feet. About five hundred of these animals exist today. They represent perhaps five percent of the total gorilla population, and while they formerly roamed far down the slopes and into the lowlands for food,

in recent years they have met civilization moving up the slopes toward them. The mountains have become their retreat, and while they are not at present in danger of extinction, conservationists are wisely taking action to set aside preserves for these mountain dwellers.

Many similar examples could be given of animals that are mountain dwellers only secondarily or that move readily from lowland realms into the mountains and then back again, their migrations controlled both by temperature and by the availability of food. But here we are concerned mainly with plants and animals that live nowhere else, adapted to those conditions that make the mountain world distinct from all other places on earth. Isolation is one of the features of the high mountains, their peaks literally like islands in the sky. The uniqueness of the plants and animals living here is a result of the high elevation. They could not exist in this rigorous environment if they had not been shaped, over countless years of evolution, specifically to meet its demands. What are some of the peculiarities of this environment? For peak and near-peak living, they must be able to tolerate less oxygen, low temperatures, high radiation, strong and persistent winds, poor soil, scarcity of food, rock slides, torrential rains, year-round drought, precipitous slopes—adversities in extreme. It is perhaps most astonishing that so many plants and animals do thrive at high altitudes. In the limited space here, only the setting and a few examples can be touched on—only enough to engender appreciation for the flora and fauna that have

Left: Meadow on Mount Rainier slope.
Right: Hardy bristlecone pine, North America.
Below: Subalpine buttercups, Washington State.
Bottom: Lupine in flower, Southern Alps,
New Zealand.

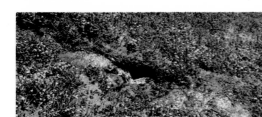

mastered the mountains as a place to live above all others.

Consider first the atmospheric pressure. Above the timberline, the air becomes rarefied—the pressure much lower than at sea level and so containing less oxygen for an equivalent volume of air. For warm-blooded animals—the birds and mammals, which need relatively large amounts of oxygen because of their high rate of metabolism—this lack of oxygen is the limiting factor that prevents invasion of the highlands by many species from below. True, a few men have climbed to more than 28,000 feet without an auxiliary oxygen supply, but discomfort due to oxygen deficiency begins for most at about 18,000 feet, or even lower. The precise level varies with individuals and with their training or conditioning, but this point is academic. It is obvious that man is not adapted for living at high altitudes. Human settlements are limited to about 15,000 feet, with some Tibetan herdsmen moving their flocks to pastures close to 17,000 feet. But some warm-blooded creatures—the true alpine dwellers—are so specifically built for life at these heights that they are uncomfortable at lower levels.

One of the most notable adaptations of alpine animals is their greater number of red blood corpuscles, making it possible for them to extract and utilize a higher percentage of oxygen from the rarefied atmosphere. In the South American Andes, for example, four members of the camel family—the llama, alpaca, guanaco, and vicuña—occupy the same highland niche as do mountain goats and wild sheep in the Northern Hemisphere. The guanaco actually lives at medium heights, as do its domesticated descendants, the llama and alpaca. But the vicuña dwells only at high elevations—10,000 feet and above. Here, in an atmosphere so thinned that man soon gasps if he tries to hurry, the vicuña moves among the clouds of the peaks at dizzying speeds. The vicuña's blood is enriched with approximately three times more red corpuscles than is a man's. The vicuña is comfortable and at home in the heights. Man is the invader.

What about very small animals? Because of their size, they are limited even in the degree to which their heart and lungs can enlarge. Shrews and rodents, the tiniest of the furry mountain dwellers, compensate for their size by having an accelerated rate of breathing and heartbeat—to about twelve hundred beats per minute in the Alpine mountain shrews of Europe and the Kenya mountain shrews of Africa. This is much faster than in lowland species, and as a result of this rapid pumping and burning of body fuels, these little animals are forced to feed almost constantly to maintain their body temperatures.

Cold is another of the limiting factors of high altitudes. The temperature decreases steadily as a slope is ascended, and the highest peaks float like icebergs in a sea of clouds. Above the timberline there are only two seasons—a winter that lasts for eight or nine months, and a short, cool summer. Temperatures fluctuate rapidly from day to night or even from hour to hour. Daytime temperatures may be high enough for plants to grow and even bloom, but at night they drop to below freezing. The surface temperature may be as much as 20 degrees below zero while plants and animals stay snugly warm in snowbanks. Great differences occur over small areas, too. One valley may be much warmer than the land above because cold winds race over it. Another, because of its position, becomes a wind trough down which the cold winds cascade. The leeward side of a rock on a sunny slope may be warm enough much of the year for a plant to grow, while on the other side—only inches away—the temperature rarely rises above freezing and the wind blows constantly at a hundred miles per hour. For plants in particular these small differences—the microclimates—are of great importance, for unlike animals, plants cannot move to find a place that is more comfortable. They must make do, if possible, wherever they start growing.

The exact boundary of the timberline is ill-defined, for plants keep pushing skyward, extending themselves to the limits of their endurance. At high elevations, trees hug the ground or crouch behind boulders. Varieties that grow tall and straight only a short distance down the slope are here prostrate and stunted, with gnarled and twisted trunks. At these high altitudes, all trees fight fierce battles against the forces of nature. On my descent to the timberline I often stop to survey these warriors in their summit battlefields, every bent tree telling a story of hardship in the heights.

Some trees are crooked and curved from the heavy loads of snow supported by their trunks and branches in the long winters. Steady winds wreak such havoc with the limbs that eventually they vanish completely on the windward side. Snow and ice polish the trunks, which may also be bleached by the sun or blackened by lightning. But even when they die, and their naked trunks turn a uniform gray, these trees remain beautiful.

In such severe conditions the bristlecone pine of North America grows. In the belt of conifers, this pine may be fifty or even sixty feet tall, but in the alpine zone it is dwarfed and amazingly persistent. Bristlecone pines growing high in the California mountains are estimated to be more than four thousand years old, the most ancient of all living things.

Mountains everywhere are famous for their flowers, for there are times when the slopes are rainbowed with color. Because of the brief growing season, most high-altitude herbaceous plants are perennials. There are plants without stems or with stems so short they offer scant surface to the swirling air masses. Most mountain flowers, from buttercups to pasqueflowers, close their petals against the cool night temperatures, then open them again at the first sign of warmth. Some even turn toward the sun. Many have adapted to their mountain life as thick, low-growing cushions, the mats helping to hold in heat. New Zealand's Alps are famous for "vegetable sheep," white woolly plants that from a distance can easily be mistaken for sheep. Totally

189

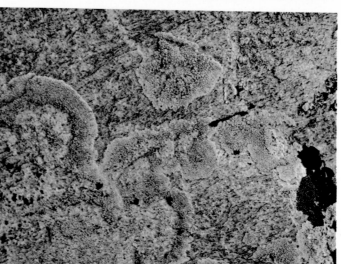

Top: Ever rarer edelweiss, Switzerland.
Above: Lichen, High Sierras, California.
Left: Yellow willow, red bearberry, Mount McKinley.
Right: Wildflowers at 12,000 ft (3,658 m), Bolivia.

unrelated plants become startling look-alikes, the demands of the environment dictating their growth habits. Often they bear little resemblance to lowland relatives that may be tall and gangly. Many alpine plants have roots as much as two feet long but can afford an above-ground exposure of only an inch or two, and their growth each year is imperceptible. Some may not bloom for years and then produce a profusion of flowers that turn the mountain landscape into a veritable riot of color. Again, temperature is a controlling factor. On low slopes, most wildflowers bloom in spring, but on the high slopes—at 10,000 feet and above—blooming does not occur until much later, and like the bodies of the plants, the flowers are tiny.

The edelweiss of the Swiss Alps is perhaps the most celebrated of all alpine wildflowers, feted in song and poem. This star-shaped beauty, pure white with gold dots, blooms from July through September, but it is now rare, a victim primarily of travelers who cannot resist picking the flowers or, worse, uprooting the entire plant. Edelweiss is now protected by law, and stiff fines are meted to those caught molesting it. Nevertheless, botanists predict that Swiss edelweiss will be extinct within a few years. Other species of edelweiss grow in the high mountains of Siberia and Japan. In their natural habitat, the edelweiss flowers are strikingly handsome, startling jewels in the snow and rocks. But removed from these surroundings and contrasted with lowland species, the harsh features that make their survival possible at high elevations

stand out starkly. They are tough-stemmed plants covered with a whitish wool, even on their leaves, and while the flowers are attractive, they are not outstandingly so except in their natural setting. Nature's beauties are best appreciated on the composite canvas, left in place and undisturbed.

Plants do not stop at the scraggly edge of the coniferous forest band. Higher up, on the treeless tundra or alpine zone, are grasses, sedges, and miniature flowering herbs, and along the streams are thickets of alders, willows, or birches, becoming dwarfed and scattered toward the peak.

Pioneers of these treeless, wind-swept lands are the lichens. Consisting of two kinds of lower plants, an alga and a fungus growing in mutualism, the crusty, cushiony, and sometimes leaflike lichens sprawl over bare rocks, their colors ranging from red or brown to silvery gray or green. Acids produced by their growth contribute to the slow erosion of the rocks, aiding the mechanical processes that also break apart the rocks. In summer, for example, the sun blisters a rock's surface while the core remains extremely cold. The sharply contrasted temperatures cause the rock surface to scale or flake. Moisture that seeps into tiny cracks or crevices freezes, and the powerful wedging effect splits a rock or breaks off pieces. These forces work with the lichens year after year. The debris accumulates, with organic matter added from the lichens and from materials carried in by the winds from below. Eventually a tiny pocket of soil forms in which

Left: Resourceful, adaptable yak, Himalayas.
Below: Ethereal snow leopard, Pakistan.
Middle l: Briefly active frog, High Sierras.
Middle r: Hoary marmot, Tetons, Wyoming.
Bottom: European salamander needs humidity on high.

mosses or miniature herbaceous plants grow.

Primitive plants grow even on the snowfields of the peaks. A green alga that surrounds itself with a reddish gelatinous coat sometimes spreads rampantly over wide areas and turns the white surface pinkish, a phenomenon known as "red snow" and one of the most striking of the alpine region. At the same time, tucked into warm beds of snow sometimes several feet deep, many other plants bide their time waiting for the first thaw, then burst into bloom even while the whiteness of winter still surrounds them. Yellow buttercups (pure gold on white), crocuses, primroses, bilberries, poppies, gentians—one can only marvel at their hardiness. In the North American Rockies, thousands of vivid yellow avalanche lilies push through the snow, their delicate petals and blossoms surprising the mountain traveler. Oddly, these plants need protection not only from cold but also from the intense sunlight of the high elevations. Some wear miniature parasols of hairs or are covered with layers of fine wool, and many have waxy leaves. These features help to shield the plants from radiation as well as to hold in heat and moisture.

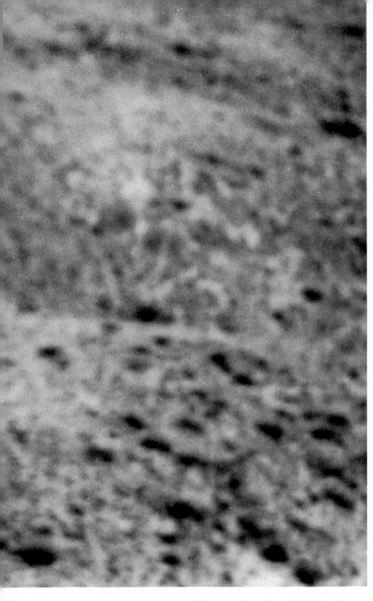

Alpine animals—that is, those that do not move to lower regions in winter— survive the low temperatures of the heights by various means. Many escape winter by hibernating. Hidden in burrows or deep rocky crevices, they curl themselves into furry balls and enter a state of torpor, seeming to teeter on the very threshold of death as their metabolic processes slow almost to a standstill. Their bodies subsist on the fat accumulated during the summer months of heavy feeding. Mice, marmots, and other rodents that live in the cold of high mountains are hibernators, many of them moving down to the timberline before beginning their winter sleep. The few kinds of amphibians and reptiles that have invaded the heights are also hibernators. Insects pass the winter in some resting stage of their life cycle.

Large animals that stay at the heights must simply brave the cold in some manner. Tibetan gazelles and chirus scrape out trenches in which they lie to avoid bitterly cold winds. But of all the warm-blooded animals, none is better suited for survival in the cold than the yak, which lives on the Tibetan plateau at 15,000 feet and higher. The yak cannot, in fact, survive in lowlands. When explorer Sven Hedin visited the Himalayas early in the 1900s, the yaks were still frighteningly wild beasts, but today many are domesticated, making robust companions for mountain farmers and nomadic tribes. A yak can carry heavy loads, climb steep slopes, and walk sure-footedly across fast streams. It provides meat and milk, cheese and butter; its fat yields fuel for lamps, its hide leather for shoes and clothing. Its bushy tail becomes an ornament in a monastery. Even its dung is used—dried, it is an excellent fuel for fires. The yak's thick, shaggy coat and dense underfur give it protection in temperatures that not uncommonly dip to 40 degrees below zero. Herds of these powerfully built beasts roam the highlands feeding on the sparse

Left: Ground-dwelling willow ptarmigan has adapted to alpine life zone. Top: James's flamingo is native to Andes elevations. Above: Golden (l) and bald eagles are strong fliers capable of functioning in high winds.

grasses and sedges. Often the yaks are forced to dig through deep snow to make a meal of crusty lichens, and sometimes they may go for many days with no food at all.

Sharing the Himalayas with the yak is the only truly alpine cat—the snow leopard, which wears a thick, soft, gray coat. Any large predator is hard pressed to find food in the mountain heights. A full-grown yak, which may weigh as much as a ton, is quite a formidable adversary even for these big cats, but yak calves, ibexes, and other smaller animals make satisfying meals. It is unfortunate that the handsome fur of these rare cats has made them the target of hunters. Perhaps fewer than a hundred now exist, for though they are protected by law, their pelts still somehow make their way to markets.

That birds inhabit mountain heights is a bit surprising, but many kinds have adapted to mountain life. They have the advantage of flight, which enables them to move quickly away from suddenly intolerable conditions and to span large territories in their constant quest for food. A great many are transients, appearing high on the slopes in summer but departing as soon as winter winds begin. Because of the unusually high velocity of the winds, perching birds are not common in the mountains. Ground dwellers, like the ptarmigans, and strong fliers, like the eagles and swifts, are most suited for alpine conditions. Earthcreepers, which belong to the same family as lowland ovenbirds, master the cold of the Andes by digging tunnels as much as three feet long, in which they lay their eggs. Wallcreepers, relatives of the common nuthatches that feed on insects on the bark of trees, hunt for insects on rocky cliffs in their mountain habitats in Europe and Asia. They move over sheer rock faces or flutter out, butterflylike, to catch insects in midair. They make their nests in deep crevices, lining them with grass and moss. But in winter, the wallcreepers typically move down the slopes to find warmth.

Accentors are small bunting-like birds widespread in the mountains of Europe, Asia, and Africa. They are ground feeders, like towhees and finches, and in winter they move down the slopes where they can still find food. Snow finches are the sparrows of the alpine region, nesting at 5,000 feet and higher in the Alps and other European mountains and as high as 15,000 feet in the Himalayas. Alpine choughs belong to the same family as crows, jays, and ravens and resemble them in all features except their slim, curved bills. Flocks of choughs have been observed at heights of more than five miles in the Himalayas. Along alkaline lakes high in the Andes, flocks of flamingos are a startling sight, but this is the home of both the Andean and James's flamingo. It is surprising, too, that many hummingbirds inhabit only high altitudes—from 10,000 to 20,000 feet. The giant hummingbird measures more than eight inches long, a good example of large size as a characteristic of high-altitude dwellers. Unlike other hummingbirds, whose wings beat so rapidly they cannot be seen—as much as two hundred beats per second—the giant hummingbird flaps its wings so slowly that they are still clearly visible as the bird flies.

With a wingspan exceeding ten feet—greater than any other living bird—the Andean condor is the most magnificent of all birds. Its unusual means of takeoff and flight provide an excellent example of adaptation to mountain conditions. Because of its huge size, the condor is unable simply to take off and fly as smaller lowland birds do; it is too big and heavy to generate the necessary speed or to leap into the air and stay aloft by means of initially hard, rapid wingbeats. Instead, it jumps off the edge of a cliff or ledge or similar aerie and rides the mountain's strong thermals. Once airborne, it can soar for hours, high above the loftiest peaks, in its search for food. Like the closely related and nearly as large California condor, it is a carrion eater. Both of these giants are endangered species. Their reproductive rates are low, the females laying only one egg every other year and the young totally dependent on its parent for at least a year. Most devastating has been the slaughter of these big birds by man, for no better reason than the sport of killing them. Occupying the same niche in the Alps in Europe is the bearded vulture, or lammergeyer, a kite that feeds on carrion. In fact, the lammergeyer eats vulture leftovers, carrying big bones hundreds of feet into the air and then dropping them on rocks to break them open so they can get at the marrow. Lammergeyers and vultures ride the thermals of the mountains, soaring from sunup to sundown with scarcely a flap of their wings. Lammergeyers have been seen at heights exceeding 30,000 feet.

Sharing the mountain skies with the vultures are eagles and hawks. Some have retreated to the mountains as a last stronghold; for others, the mountains have always been their home. Among these is the golden eagle, the most regal of the clan. Many hawks migrate in winter, not in solid groups or flocks, but singly along the same corridors over ridges and through mountain passes, where air currents keep them moving swiftly.

Just as the strong winds make the mountains precarious for many kinds of birds, the winds are also a limiting factor in determining the kinds of insects that can live high in the mountains. At times the mountaintops may swarm with insects and spiders, but most of these have been carried up by the winds from lower levels. They are not residents of the heights and do not survive long there. Most of the truly alpine insects are flightless. The thick-bodied grasshoppers, wingless or nearly so, are clad densely with "hair." Butterflies are scarce but are conspicuous because of their flight. They beat their wings rapidly and stay close to the surface where the wind is not as strong. When it is very cold—even on summer mornings in the alpine region—the butterflies and the few other kinds of flying insects sometimes have difficulty getting started, but once they are flying, their muscles generate enough heat to keep them on the move. Adult butterflies, which have thick "hairy" bodies, live only a few weeks. They overwinter either as eggs or pupae under rocks or in similar protected places. A

201

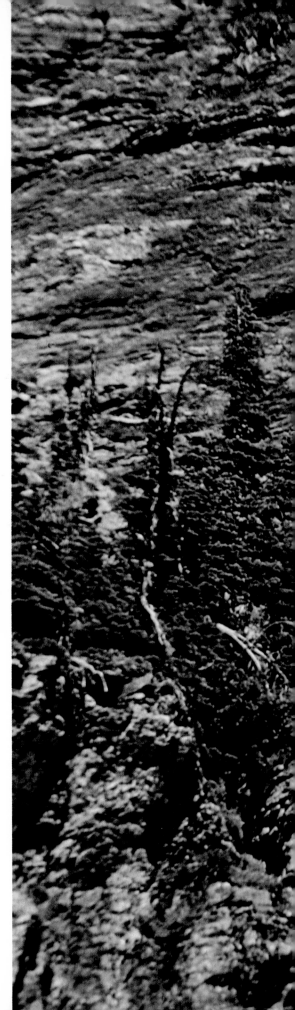

*High-leaping, sharp-horned
Alpine chamois (above)
is in goat-antelope category.
Bighorns (r) of western
U.S. are true sheep. Despite
inaccessibility of their
habitat, they are under
pressure from trophy hunters,
disease, and other
intrusions of civilization.*

202

Ibex species have been hunted
nearly to extinction for presumed aphrodisiac
qualities of horns. Following pages:
Rocky Mountain goat's well-designed
hooves are ideal for meager mountain ledges.

few kinds are so precisely adapted to their high-altitude existence that their eggs will not hatch or their pupae will not transform if transported to lower levels.

In number of species, however, insects are the most abundant animals of the alpine region. Almost all are active only during the day. At night they become stiff with cold, but a touch of the sun is enough to stir them to life again. Most numerous are the collembolans or springtails, those living in the alpine region generally referred to as snowfleas. They abound even on snow and ice and have been recorded at elevations above 20,000 feet. Most of them are dark blue or black, and they sometimes occur in such large numbers that they appear to color the snow. As with all insects living at these heights, scarcity of food limits their numbers and distribution. Collembolans feed on a variety of organic matter but mainly on pollen blown up the slopes from the coniferous forests.

Typically, the mountain peaks are humid, for they are wrapped in dense blankets of clouds at all times. Thick fogs finger down the valleys. The highest rainfall recorded in the world is on Mount Waialeale on the island of Kauai in Hawaii. It exceeds 450 inches annually and may be nearly 490, making these slopes the wettest place on earth. Mountains are literally rainmakers, for as warm air from the lowlands rises and cools, it cannot hold its moisture, and loses it either as rain or snow. On the slopes, the water moves downward rapidly, eroding the soil and washing the rocks bare. If it falls as snow at the peak, it builds the white cap from which glaciers and avalanches slide downward. Not unusually, all of the precipitation falls on only one side of a mountain. The other side is arid, swept by cold, dry winds. The broad, cold Tibetan plateau in the Himalayas is a cold desert produced in this manner. The flora and fauna on one side of a mountain must be adapted to moist conditions, even torrential downpours and flooding, while those on the other must be equipped for survival in a cold, windy desert.

Most alpine animals are dark in color—or at least darker than their nearest relatives or even members of the same species that live at lower altitudes. The dark color has survival value, for it not only absorbs heat more readily but also protects the animals from the higher concentration of ultraviolet rays in the rarefied atmosphere. Some animals change color with the season—white in winter, dark in summer. Ptarmigans, weasels, and snowshoe hares go through these seasonal changes, their colors also helping to camouflage them and give protection from predators.

Two animals whose coloration does not conform to this general pattern are the Dall sheep of Alaska and northwestern Canada and the North American mountain goat, both of which are white year-round. Because both animals tend to live either high enough or far enough north so that they are always surrounded by some snow, their white coats provide good camouflage even in midsummer.

Steepness makes a mountain.

Many rises at high elevations are nearly vertical walls of bare rock. Where the slopes are not sheer, they are generally covered with rock debris from slides and sometimes almost steady flows of rocks from above. All of the animals inhabiting these rocky areas must be alert to the danger of falling rocks. They must be sure-footed and agile, capable also of leaping from one precipice to another. Throughout the Northern Hemisphere, this niche is filled by different species of wild sheep and goats. Their two front toes are pincerlike for grasping rocky prominences, and unlike other mammals of their order, they lower their entire foot as they climb, so that even their dew claws dig in to give them a firm hold.

Goats are typically bearded and have a distinctive odor produced by glands on their face and feet. Most of them have long saberlike horns, curved upward and often spiraled, but never projecting to the sides as in sheep. The best known of the wild goats are the half-dozen species of ibexes. The Alpine ibex was once common throughout the Alps but was hunted to near extinction for its handsome sickle-shaped horns, which grow to more than three feet long, and because various parts of its body were believed valuable as medicines and aphrodisiacs. Only a few dozen animals still existed when one Italian family placed them under rigid protection on their private preserve. Eventually governments also set aside parks where the animals could be protected. Breeding stock was obtained from the Italian family's herd, and now the population is estimated to be in excess of ten thousand. The markhor is a heavy-bodied wild goat inhabiting the Himalayas. Its horns are short, heavy, and spiraled. Also living in the Himalayas is the tahr, which has a long, shaggy coat. It is not a true goat, lacking odor glands and having much smaller horns.

The so-called goat-antelopes are a special group that fit midway between true goats and sheep. Included are the takins, serows, and gorals of the Himalayas, but the two best known goat-antelopes are the chamois of the Alps and the Rocky Mountain goats of western North America. The chamois' horns measure less than a foot long, are sharp-pointed, and curve down at their tips. Mark Twain paralleled the flea and the chamois because of their ability to make extremely high jumps—the chamois to ten feet or more straight up and twice as far horizontally, climbing cliffs on which there is no apparent foothold and landing where there seems to be no room for its feet.

The Rocky Mountain goat is a much larger, heavier animal, but it is equally agile. Except in the most severe winter weather, it stays above the timberline, subsisting on the sparse pasturage and getting sustenance at times by munching on twigs. The elusive Rocky Mountain goat may appear suddenly on a precipice to peer down at intruders and then just as quickly be gone, moving up almost perpendicular cliffs and spanning wide chasms. Though it is uncommonly wary, it rarely appears hurried. The Rocky Mountain goat is so well adapted to the cold that even the

Left: Urial (sheep), Elburz Mountains, Iran.
Below: Tahr (goat-antelope), Himalayas, India.

211

alpine summers are sometimes too hot for its comfort, forcing it to plunge into snowbanks to get cool. Like the chamois, it has rather small horns—less than a foot long and sharp-pointed, but not curving down.

Notable among the mountain sheep is the mouflon, which lives in the mountains of central Europe. Its spiraled horns may be nearly three feet long and often curve inward at their tips. The similar and closely related urials and argalis of the Himalayas live at altitudes of 14,000 feet or higher. Argalis are the largest of all sheep, standing to four feet tall at their shoulders. The only wild sheep of the New World are the Dall and Stone sheep of Alaska and northwestern Canada and the more numerous bighorns of the western United States. The bighorn population was estimated at two million in the early days of the continent's settlement, but their numbers have been reduced to twenty thousand or fewer. Hunting was only one factor contributing to their decline. A decimating parasite transmitted by a snail is credited with causing the greatest kill, but because the snails can survive only where there is enough lime in the soil for the building of their shells, the sheep inhabiting mountains of granite rocks have been spared. Bighorns have short, heavy horns, and the rams establish territorial dominance by rushing at each other full speed and butting their heads together— not once, but again and again. The battles may last for hours before one gives up—for the time being. Apparently, neither combatant is ever seriously hurt.

Barbary sheep, or aoudads, are the only wild sheep of Africa, inhabiting the Atlas Mountains north of the Sahara. They are not true sheep, however, having long tails and more goatlike horns. The Tibetan bharal is also a sheep that has some goatlike features, including long, curved horns.

Waters of alpine lakes and streams are cold. The streams rush down the slopes, washing the pebbles and rocks on the bottom and tumbling them along until they are polished and clean. These are trout waters— fish that can swim against strong currents. Trout demand large amounts of oxygen, which is churned into the water as it moves swiftly along. Most of these high-mountain trout streams are very small, rarely measuring more than a few feet across. Salmon that come in from the sea to spawn in mountain streams do not get to this elevation.

Many of the fishes adapted for life in these rapid waters have adhesive organs with which they cling to the rocks. In some, they are formed of modified fins. The mouths of catfish living in the mountains of South America have become sucking discs with which the fish hold their position on rocks. Others hide under rocks, or they rest on the down-current side of rocks and then dart rapidly from one rock to another. Some fish, including mountain-dwelling darters and sculpins, lack swim bladders, which helps them keep close to the bottom. Their pectoral and pelvic fins are spikelike, aiding them in anchorage. Because food is not plentiful and is hard to get, the fish of high waters grow slowly and never attain large size.

The streams are inhabited also by insects. Both immature and adult forms have developed ways of anchoring themselves to rocks, or they spend their lives on the underside or down-current sides of rocks. They even fasten their eggs to rocks with a sticky secretion. In the wild, rushing torrents, these animals do not dare set out in search of food lest they be swept away themselves. Rather, they wait in quiet eddies or wherever they are well anchored for the food to be brought to them. Some spin tiny silken webs in which they catch their meals; others spread fanlike mouthparts. Caddisfly larvae live in a case made of bits of rocks glued together. The case not only camouflages them but serves also as an anchor that can be carried with them as the fragile, soft-bodied insects inside move along. Leeches, snails, and even some mussels inhabit these fast, cold waters, too. Typically, their bodies are flattened, offering a minimum of exposure and resistance in the current.

A few kinds of toads, frogs, and salamanders live in the alpine zone where the humidity is high. Because of the low temperature, they can be active only briefly, of course, but spadefoot toads and the green toad occur regularly in the Himalayas, the green toad sometimes seen as high as 15,000 feet. In the Andes, too, frogs live up to the snow line. The mouths of tadpoles of these mountain dwellers are sucking discs used for clinging to the rocks in the streams. Because of the cold, many require as long as two years or more to develop from egg to adult.

Several kinds of reptiles also live in alpine regions. Like other cold-blooded vertebrates, they are limited both by scarcity of food and by low temperature. In the Alps, the common viper, the viviparous lizard, and a blindworm range into the alpine zone. All three are viviparous. In the cold, their eggs would never hatch. In Africa, a skink that ranges up Mount Kilimanjaro to over 12,000 feet is also viviparous. In the Himalayas some species of lizards that lay eggs in the lowlands become viviparous when they invade higher elevations. Viviparous iguanid lizards are known from as high as 10,000 feet in the Andes and range northward to Mexico. Characteristic of alpine dwellers, these lizards have shorter legs than do their lowland counterparts, just as rabbits and other mammals of the alpine zone have shorter ears. Nature gives minimum exposure to appendages that might freeze.

Sadly, the mountain world of flora and fauna is no longer a sanctuary. Airplanes, helicopters, trail bikes, snowmobiles—man invades with motors as well as on foot, cutting, plucking, killing, and disrupting. Though many environmental groups are vigorously promoting awareness of and respect for high-country ecosystems, the treasures of the mountain world are still being sacked. It is shameful that we may be fast coming to a time when we can only read about or look at pictures of this wondrous world of plants and animals that used to be but is no more.

213

8

Play and Work
in the Mountains

*Preceding pages: Horse-drawn
sleigh is one of the small
pleasures of a winter visit to
Europe's ski resorts—here
in the Val Gardena of
the Dolomites. Above: Zuers,
in Austria's Vorarlberg,
offers excellent skiing, but
treasures its intimate
atmosphere, has no wish to
extend its modest dimensions.*

Once people climbed mountains only to get to the other side. Mountains were massive, imposing barriers. They were exploited for their precious metals, for the animals they hosted, and for the millions of board feet of lumber in their trees. Mastering the mountains meant using them to satisfy the wants and needs of people who lived in the valleys.

Over the years a new kind of mountain world came into being. People went to the mountains to find pleasure—to enjoy the scenery, hike the trails, climb or ski the slopes for the fun of it, fish the streams, and breathe deeply of the cool, pure air. Some people like to live as close to nature as possible when they go to the mountains. Others expect to find more than the comforts of home. They want luxury accommodations and services—and they find them, too. For those who have leisure the mountains offer recreational opportunities to satisfy every wish.

People also work in the mountains. Some mountain jobs involve helping others enjoy themselves at the resorts and parks. Other people work in the forests, aiding the preservation of the mountains as productive resources. Still others do scientific research, or service highways or communications lines, the avenues that join the mountain world with the lowlands. For most of these people the mountains are magical, compelling. Vacation visits are not satisfying. They must live there. Even those whose jobs are no different from what they might be in low country are sustained in spirit by the backdrop of the heights to which they can escape on afternoons or weekends. They find comfort in knowing that the mountains are there, and they could not imagine working anywhere but in the mountain world, their Nirvana or Shangri-la.

Tourists have brought many mountain communities to life. In 1960, mile-high Andorra, capital of the independent nation of the same name, had a population of six thousand and was barely accessible by road. Now, as a result of its discovery by tourists, this Pyrenees town has a population of twenty-five thousand. Other resorts, particularly in populated Europe, are old, mellowed by time and service. For most of these towns recreation was at first secondary, but it may be offered now in a grandiose style. Innsbruck and Grenoble both achieved importance as crossroads long before they were resorts. They were on the trade routes over the passes and served as storage depots and as way stations for couriers. Salzburg became useful in a similar way to the Romans, and there was a Chamonix as long ago as the eleventh century. Whatever their original contribution, most of these mountain communities depend now on tourists, without whom they would remain stunted, perhaps barely surviving.

Sometimes even today a traveler needs endurance to get to a particular mountain resort. From many points in central Europe, for example, it is a day's journey by train to Zermatt, high in the Swiss Alps. The locomotive strains and stutters up the steep grade from Visp to St. Niklaus to Zermatt, the end of

Preceding pages: Hikers descend slope of
the Rothorn amid spectacular scenery of Brienzer
area of Switzerland. Innsbruck's strategic
location on Alpine trade routes
preceded its prominence as a resort.

the line. At the Zermatt *bahnhof* the guest is greeted by horse-drawn hotel carriages or, as a pleasurable fillip, sleighs in winter.

For many years it was this remoteness that earned the Matterhorn region, with Zermatt as its center, its accolades as a resort. Here one could be assured of escape from the hustle and bustle of the world. Automobiles could go no further than St. Niklaus. From there an electric train lumbered uphill through tighter and tighter valleys to Zermatt, the site of the Matterhorn and the Monte Rosa. This difficult access discouraged casual visitors and transients, and made the guests who did arrive want to stay.

Motorists can find parking near Zermatt these days, but cars are still *verboten* in the town itself. Its inner sanctum—a lovely, much-photographed main street with distinguished shops and appealing old houses—remains untouched by noise and gas fumes. Its hotels have always striven for excellence. One dines well on the local *truite au bleu* (mountain trout cooked in wine) or on carefully prepared schnitzel accompanied by a Swiss white wine. Lunches can be consumed on the numerous outdoor terraces.

Visually I have always found most Alpine settlements to my liking. There is sprawling, touristy, bustling Garmisch-Partenkirchen under the Zugspitze. Not far away is Oberammergau, a tight, holy little village with serious-looking chalets set close together and decorated with religious paintings and carvings. Oberammergau comes to life

only once every ten years, when it stages the Passion Play.

Remoteness keeps the number of visitors to these communities relatively low, but local attitude also slows growth. Some resorts work at preserving their original character as much as possible. After all, this is what attracted people in the first place. Zuers, for instance, is a skier's paradise. All other winter sports take a back seat and there is little resort activity the rest of the year. What about the possibility of growth?

At lunch one day, a Zuers city father opened my eyes. He pointed to the gaps between local hotels. "Americans would fill those spaces," he commented, while we ate our liver-dumpling soup. "But *should* they build so much? Perhaps not." He then told me that the people of Zuers had made a joint decision not to sell land to anyone, at any price, under any circumstances. They had concluded that Zuers needs no further expansion. Twelve hundred beds are enough. The hotels are always full in season and the lifts work to capacity. Besides, in some locations new buildings would stand in the path of avalanches.

As we dug into our Viennese pastries, he added, "If a new hotel goes up, it means that we must install more ski lifts, too. And why? To bring even more people? To destroy the intimate character of Zuers?" Good question.

The same rationale may apply in a different way to nearby St. Christoph, a few simple houses and hostelries sitting on the

220

knees of bulky mountains. St. Christoph fills another sort of niche. It is the site of the Austrian Federal Sports School, where well-worn classrooms turn out future skiing instructors. Every certified skiing instructor in Austria must pass a stiff final exam at St. Christoph, and Austrians look up to this specialized school in the way young American physicists do to M.I.T. At St. Christoph, the most difficult and demanding institution of its kind in the world, students concentrate on all facets of their sport. For 184 days, over two successive winters, they spend hours on the slopes learning all the fine points of technique, and, in the classrooms, take courses in such subjects as anatomy, the physics of motion, geology, glaciology, and botany. They are required to know about the origin and composition of rocks, the various shapes of ice crystals, trees and wildflowers, cloud formations, and weather patterns. They also learn at least two foreign languages and are trained in advanced first aid. To change St. Christoph in any way would be to destroy it.

The Arlberg's larger and better-known centers, like St. Anton, have had their share of development. But the towns controlled their architects and contractors. As a result, St. Anton remains charmingly Tyrolean, despite new housing. The narrow main street is made up of impressive old chalets. Newer Alpine chalets, as almost anywhere in the Austrian mountains, are white stucco, the façades adorned by artists in red, deep brown, or black wood. Staircases are hand-hewn; the roofs jut and slope protectively. The ornate balconies stand out with their long flower boxes. Like the houses, shops in the Arlberg are designed with care. Their signs are always artistic, with deft uses made of copper, tin, and wrought iron.

A large vacation center, such as St. Anton or the more strung-out Kitzbühel, makes an attempt to amuse the assorted customers after dinner. St. Anton night life percolates for all tastes. A mountain town's ambience always depends on who goes there. The people who frequent St. Anton or Kitzbühel care more for entertainment than do those who go to Lech, Oberlech, Stuben, and other small Austrian villages. Zuers hosts kings, queens, princes, shahs, diplomats—most of whom wish to holiday undisturbed.

Crowds may change with the season, too. The height of winter turns Badgastein, Austria, into a ski-racing center, with its two-mile-long Fédération Internationale de Ski (FIS) downhill run matching the precipitous angle of Badgastein's waterfall. In late spring the waterfall melts and cascades through the center of the city. A new wave of guests, much older than the skiers, arrives. Spa in action! In summer, Badgastein is indeed a town for baths —mineral baths, even mouth baths. The mountain water supposedly brings relief to chronic gum conditions. Large hotels have their own thermal baths and special drinking fountains. Badgastein doctors are on hand to prescribe a regime of miraculous waters, a light diet, enough mountain air, and gentle walks—daily doses of *spazieren gehen*. If St. Anton is Tyrolean

rustic, then Badgastein is forever Grand Hotel —several, in fact, keeping the total of about six thousand beds filled year-round. Some of the hostelries are as ancient as Badgastein's eighteen radioactive springs. Europe's royalty was familiar with these waters even in medieval times, but the big boom began around the turn of the twentieth century, when the first palatial hotels were built.

Across a few mountain passes and the Austrian border is the even busier mountain resort of St. Moritz, with grand hotels and correspondingly grand prices. As early as the sixteenth century, physicians knew of the health wonders of the Engadine, the long valley of the Inn River, and organized winter activities at St. Moritz go back more than a hundred years, when vacationers began flocking to the Upper Engadine by sleigh. Skating became popular, and curling, known in Scotland since the sixteenth century, also invaded St. Moritz. The Cresta toboggan run was built in the 1880s, and the bobsled soon made its appearance, too.

An Olympics center as well, St. Moritz sprawls at the base of the Pi Corvatch (11,130 ft/3,392 m) and the Diavolezza, a thousand feet lower. Tramways are distributed over various sections of the metropolis, but one needs good legs or a good car to get from place to place here. St. Moritz regulars outdo one another with fine automobiles, creating excessive traffic that moves on many levels above, below, and around the city.

St. Moritz is not a simple, compact place like St. Christoph. It is not exactly suited to intimacy, and both winter and summer seasons are hectic. Has St. Moritz changed over the years? Hardly. The resort remains the flamboyant, fashion-conscious, snobbish, and truly sophisticated *grande dame* of the world's mountain resorts. It caters to the rich and the beautiful, to international conductors and playwrights, to sex symbols and jet-setters, to royalty, movie stars, and café society, along with their entourages. St. Moritz is a fascinating mountain resort where the mountains have somehow come to play only a minor role.

Davos is Switzerland's largest mountain resort, its population varying from eleven thousand to twenty-five thousand depending on the month. It takes an hour to walk the length of the traffic-choked and pedestrian-congested main street. Davos is the family spot for Europeans, with dozens of little hotels and *pensions* scattered above the town. The crowds here speak many languages, with German predominating. From dawn to dusk, summer and winter, the famous Parsenn-bahn hoists hundreds of people up to the Weissfluh, shuttling the scenery watchers and wanderers along with the skiers. Davos is for children, too. In summer there is horseback riding across the flowered meadows, rock climbing, guided nature walks, and junior tennis. In winter, the young people twirl and dash about on skates in an international ice rink. They go "ski-bobbing," too, which is biking on skis, and they swim in the gargantuan Hallenbad or hike on special trails that are kept snow-free all year. Some families

*Zermatt (top) is an old Swiss mountain
village overlaid by a ski town. St. Christoph and
St. Anton (below l & r) are great centers of
Austrian ski culture, tradition, and
instruction. Peak behind St. Christoph is Valluga.*

toboggan or hop onto buses for rides through the valley. One can watch all kinds of ski races, marked by fierce speed, wild jumps, and sensational falls. The congestion of Davos's narrow pedestrian walks, the filled outdoor cafés, the morning queues at the lower lift terminals—all are forgiven when one immerses himself in the vast mountain acreage of the Parsenn ski area.

Anyone who has ever taken the Davos-Parsenn run will never forget it. An older or slower skier may need a whole afternoon to get down the Parsenn. The sharpness of the village roofs and balconies etched against the sparkling slopes still stands out in my own mind after such a run. I remember with pleasure how I skied through pastures and forests, through farmyards and down village paths. I overtook farmers in their sleighs and passed Swiss children returning home from school, their tiny skis clattering and their square book sacks bouncing on their little shoulders. On other stretches I was alone. On a knoll I caught my breath to watch the curve of immense slopes grinning from across the valley, clear white dotted with farms and occasional chalets. The Parsenn's various *pistes* lead down to Klosters and other communities.

Including the alfresco lunch stop at a restaurant en route, the run to Küblis took me three hours. On the brief train trip from there to Davos, the starting point of the adventure, I checked the elevations and distances on my map. I had skied nearly twenty kilometers and dropped almost 7,000 feet (2,134 m) from the Parsenn summit. No one could ask for more.

Certain French mountain villages are architecturally advanced, unique in their conception. Some of them were tailored for the coming century, built into Alpine nests by architects who are passionate about novelty and *le style futuristique*. Avoriaz, for example, represents the combined efforts of three young French architects who created a collection of terraced beehives. Abby Rand, a well-known travel writer, reported, "The Avoriaz effect is very nervous, all jutting planes and aggressive angles—a fleet of ships straining at their moorings."

Cars must stay at lower elevations at Avoriaz. They have also been kept out of Flaine, a resort complex two hours from Geneva. Conceived by a Parisian industrialist, Flaine was planned so that one can walk to any point. A noted architect designed Flaine's futuristic housing, which comes as a surprise up there in the wilderness, all gray concrete with slits and angular balconies. The hotels, with their powerful, serious façades, look like U.S. embassy buildings transplanted to the French Alps. But the strange architectural experience is made up for by the superlative skiing. Some fifteen thousand snowy acres make for an invigorating, ego-building vacation. From the crests one sees Mont Blanc.

Many holiday colonies in the mountain world are well conceived. The planners of Aviemore Centre, a resort built in 1966 between Perth and Inverness in the Scottish Highlands, chose their location with care. Avie-

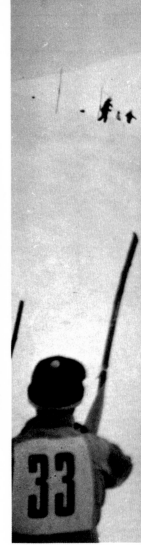

Half a World Apart: "Flying Mile" (below) is a favorite downhill run on Mont Tremblant, the Laurentians' highest. Russians (opposite) on slopes of Alatau Mountains of Central Asia, near Olympic training site at Alma-Ata.

more has direct train and bus connections with the major cities of England and Scotland, an important factor in the British Isles. Winter snows are guaranteed in the 2,000-foot Cairngorm Mountains. Investors gambled on the increased leisure time of the British and Scots middle class to assure them of customers, and their calculations were correct. Aviemore Centre quickly became Scotland's most important mountain resort, a financial success by any standard. The Cairngorms are covered with birch forests and belt-high ferns, adorned by quiet ponds, full of soothing little brooks and bird songs. Trails go hither and thither and allow a few rock scrambles to spots where one can survey the pleasant Spey valley, whose river provides water for the manufacture of much fine Scotch whisky. A few miles from Scotland's up-to-date resort the heather blooms.

A decade ago, Canada's mild and beguiling Laurentians were still mostly a four-season playground for people from nearby Montreal. Only a few outsiders filtered in, but now these little mountains are dotted with private chalets in pastel shades as well as small guesthouses and hotels. The Laurentians have become a popular year-round vacation region,

boasting French and Swiss innkeepers, interesting bistros and boutiques. As you drive north from Montreal, the village names roll off your tongue: St. Jérôme, Ste. Adèle-en-Haut, St. Sauveur, Ville d'Esterel, La Belle Neige! From the lodges, hiking trails wander through forests to scenic outlooks, circle a number of ponds, and lead past abandoned huts. Laurentian slopes have become a favorite with skiers, too, the connoisseurs heading for the resort at the base of Mont Tremblant—at 3,500 feet (1,067 m) the region's altitude champion. In winter it can get bitter cold, with snow aplenty. Ice skaters and curlers are out anyway, and the hos-

telries are comfortable. One eats well here. Quebec's French-Canadian food combines the delicacy, sensitivity, and imagination of French cuisine with generous North American portions.

In western North America, the mountains were first a land of mystery, and their exploration by such pioneers as Lewis and Clark thrilled the budding nation. The explorers were followed by hunters, trappers, prospectors, lumbermen—people who were mainly seeking fortunes in the mountains. Other men of the mountains were geographers, like Ferdinand Hayden, and explorer-naturalists, like

229

*Scientific Research in the Rockies: Atop Niwot
Ridge, northwest of Boulder, INSTAAR, the University
of Colorado's Institute of Arctic and Alpine
Research, is conducting year-round environmental
studies. Opposite: Researcher changes graph
of anemometer twirling at 12,300-ft (3,749-m) altitude.
Above: Checking monitor that measures and
records incoming solar and atmospheric radiation,
and that reflected back from earth's surface.*

Australian power lines climb Snowy Mountains of New South Wales, while "Cat" bulldozes road and railway route over Andes between Chile and Argentina. Now completed, road runs by scenic natural bridge, railway through two-mile tunnel.

John Muir. They were at home among the peaks and rock slabs that some authorities pronounced unfit for habitation. These frontiersmen, always on the move, opened up the mountains. Today people play where once the heights were only a forbidding wilderness.

In the U.S. Rockies, some of today's prominent year-round resorts began as mining camps, and an effort has been made to preserve their authenticity. In Colorado, for example, Crested Butte's main street and its rows of rugged little shops have not changed greatly in the last century. Space had no premium in the early days, so the width of the street is remarkable. Even the new buildings match the old style pretty well and still suit their purpose at the 8,000-foot (2,438-m) elevation. A few outlying guesthouses and motels take care of hunters, hikers, and cross-country skiers, and somewhat higher up there is a well-developed ski area with its own world of lifts, lodges, eateries, and condominiums. Aspen and Breckinridge are two other Colorado resorts that started as mining towns. In Utah, Alta's ski lodges are in a deep, narrow canyon where the diggings and pilings of miners are still in evidence.

Other big-time resorts have a prior history of agriculture or logging. Whistler Mountain, in British Columbia, was timber country before becoming a Canadian ski station. The Canadian railroad chiefs created Banff, in Alberta, when they started building large hotels there, and giant Banff National Park, established in 1885, completed the resort.

The cool summers and the snow-rich winters soon attracted guests from Toronto and the Canadian provinces.

Tiny Squaw Valley began as an agricultural "gem" in California's Sierra Nevada, at 6,126 feet (1,867 m) above sea level. The farmers raised hay and churned butter and cheese, which found a ready market among sawmill workers and the little hotels around Lake Tahoe. Now Squaw Valley is a major resort area and famous as the site of the 1960 Winter Olympics. A magnificent group of peaks, bowls, and glades form the backdrop for a complex of large lodges, hotels, private homes, sports arenas, and various other facilities for guests.

Sun Valley, Idaho, another western mountain mecca, owes its existence to the railroad barons. Sun Valley's founders sent a French count across the mountains of North America in search of the perfect resort site. In his footsteps followed a publicity wizard who suggested that Sun Valley should be done "on a big scale, with class and snap." It was, too, with the assistance of competent architects who designed a complete Alpine village instead of just some scattered motels. Sun Valley was planned by people with foresight. There are no neon lights, no ghost houses, and no automobiles on the main street. Even today, some forty years later and after plenty of expansion, one is struck by the freshness and attractiveness of this village. Sun Valley remains a remote and difficult-to-reach enclave. The surrounding central Idaho mountains look like brown potato

Tasks on High Mountains: Opposite (from top),
U.S. Forest ranger monitors weather gauges in Colorado,
Forest Service crew replants cutover area in Montana,
student firefighters prepare for real thing. Below:
Fire lookout in Helena National Park, Montana.

sacks in summer, white flour sacks in winter.

Many of the jobs in the mountains are related directly to these playgrounds, for vacationers need food, transportation, entertainment, guides—a multitude of services. The diversity of jobs in the mountains is as great as in the lowlands. But the unique qualities of the heights and the wilderness also require special kinds of work, and there are occupations in the mountains that can be found nowhere else. The New Zealand pilot who takes sightseers, climbers, and skiers to the glaciers, the Austrian ski instructors at work in Japanese mountain resorts, the guides in the Wyoming Tetons—the list is long, and many of these people would not consider working anywhere but in the mountain world.

Some scientists go to the summits for their research. As early as 1870, meteorologists staffed a weather observatory atop Mount Washington in New Hampshire. For the past fifty years, in a summit observatory on Kilauea Crater on the island of Hawaii, scientists have monitored the volcano's behavior, charting its "pulse" with a variety of sensitive instruments. They measure the temperature and the pressure of gases, sample the rocks, study earthquakes and the magnetic field of the volcano. From such research the world is learning not only more about this mountain but also about others like it around the world.

Other scientific detectives on Mauna Loa measure the world's air pollution, and physicists delve into research on cosmic rays from a pinnacle in the Rockies. Many of these men of science confide that the magnetism of the mountains is such an inexorable force that they could never be happy in flat country.

Biologists, too, find fascinating work in the mountain world, the slopes offering an abundant variety of life conditions and habitats in only a short distance. From a 1½-mile-high vantage point 25 miles north of Boulder, Colorado, Dr. Michael Grant heads several projects of Colorado University's Institute for Arctic and Alpine Research. He monitors the water qualities of mountain brooks, compares the protein content of gnarled trees at the timberline with those farther down the slopes, measures the growth rate of minuscule flowers of the tundra, and devotes months to trapping field mice, marking and cataloguing them, and then releasing them for recapture in a follow-up survey later. Dr. Grant's research seeks pure knowledge. From it will come a better understanding of life and living conditions not only in the high country but throughout the biotic world. Transplanted from the moist lowlands of the South himself, Dr. Grant works in the mountains by preference, exhilarated by the heights and challenged by the research possibilities offered by the mountain world.

A pockmarked rocky road leads to the simple cabins and sheds of the mountain research station from which, for almost twenty years, climatologist John Clark has traveled to and from his four weather stations, among North America's highest points for monitoring wind velocities, solar radiation, precipitation, temperatures, and other data. John Clark

237

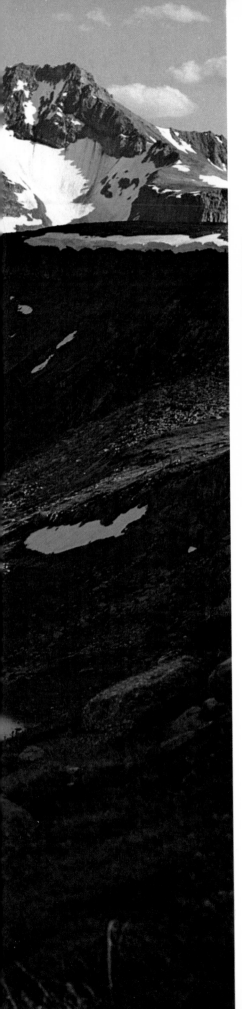

Opposite: A ride through the splendor of the Canadian Rockies. Left: U.S. Bureau of Land Management agent checks mountain boundaries with map in the field. Below: Snug camper-climber bedded down in ice cave.

239

works in a high-altitude situation by choice, braving hardships he would not have to face elsewhere. Almost every winter trees crash into power lines, causing outages that may last ten to fifteen hours, plunging the entire research station into sudden darkness. Cold spreads through the laboratories, endangering the delicate equipment. The drilling cold on these mountain ridges forced Clark to design special sheds for the gas heaters in his labs above timberline. He uses Jeeps, cross-country skis, tracked vehicles, and even snowshoes to reach his strip-chart recorders and anemometers, which require his year-round attention. But John Clark would not work anywhere else, despite the problems. He is a mountain man.

As I wandered from peak to peak in Europe several summers ago, I got acquainted with the hardy Alpine types in charge of the high mountain huts. Hikers can spend a night and buy a modest meal in such outposts before setting out for the next valley. There are hundreds of these huts—*hutten* or *refugios*—each manned by a caretaker who has a special fondness for the ridges and stone waves that encircle him. These men are modern-day counterparts of the monks of the Middle Ages who, with their giant St. Bernard dogs, manned hospices that saved many a wayfarer's life.

Mountain people do have that kind of concern for those who venture into their world. When snow sends people to the slopes to ski, many unwisely and unknowingly put themselves right in the path of the dreaded "White Death," killer avalanches that hang on the mountainsides poised and ready to come thundering down. It was to cope with this constant threat that the U.S. Forest Service created the special job of snow ranger some forty years ago in the Wasatch National Forest at Alta, Utah. More than a hundred people had lost their lives in avalanches at Alta even before the community became a resort. Now there were people coming to the mountains who had had no experience at all with these white monsters, and so did not know enough to fear them.

Mountain people reasoned wisely that the only way to deal with the danger was to attack first. The U.S. Forest Service organized its unique corps of snow rangers to wage war on the masses of snow and ice when they threatened and to serve as guardians for those who came to the slopes for fun. Today the snow rangers do their work not only at Wasatch National Forest but in every snow-covered mountain recreation area in the Forest Service's domain. Dressed in green parkas marked with bright yellow shoulder patches, the snow rangers are symbols of safety, assurances that ski trips will not become tragedies.

Before he can assume the responsibilities of being a snow ranger, a man must prove himself in training programs comparable to those at the ski-instructor school at St. Christoph in Austria. He must, of course, be an expert skier and in excellent physical condition, able to withstand the rigors of any emergency situation. He must be a mountaineer through and through, familiar with all aspects of the high country. He must know about the winds and the weather and, most important, about avalanches—what starts them and how they can be forced to spend themselves before they become killers. He masters the art of shooting them down with a 75-mm recoilless rifle, blasting them off their perches with TNT, or even skiing them off the slopes, a delicate and dangerous technique requiring superb skill to keep from getting caught in the roaring slides himself.

Above all, the snow ranger must understand and like people. He must enjoy helping them have fun—even those who do not appreciate that his labor is in their behalf. His job is not easy, the workday starting before dawn. By starlight and with the thermometer at its lowest, the snow ranger makes his first check on the day's weather. A foot of new snow, a shift in the wind, a change in the temperature—a new day means a different set of conditions on the mountains, perhaps ripening the slopes for avalanches. The snow ranger must be sure the slopes are safe before allowing skiers to venture onto them.

As a safety measure, snow rangers work in pairs when shooting down avalanches. Members of the National Ski Patrol, an organization of dedicated volunteers, are also called on when it seems advisable to go over the slopes carefully before opening them for the day. With a partner, the snow ranger begins firing his 75-mm rifle. Lodge visitors are jolted out of bed by the familiar sound of this "alarm clock" as it reverberates through the valleys. Avalanches tumble down the mountains, cheated of making surprise slides on unsuspecting skiers later in the day. Then the snow rangers and the volunteer patrolmen go over the slopes one by one to determine which can be opened and which must be left closed, at least until inspected more carefully. Working from the top, the rangers test the big slopes by tossing out blocks of TNT to see if the explosions dislodge avalanches. The rangers and patrolmen ski the smaller slopes. All of this must be done with speed, for in the lodges, the skiers

241

are already getting their gear together. The snow rangers are charged with their safety, and they do not take the responsibility lightly.

All day long the snow rangers are on duty, always ready to respond to any needs, but also participating in a variety of sessions with other rangers and administrators. There may be plans to open new slopes, to add new lifts, or to make other changes in the resort complex and its multiple-use offerings. Always, too, there are new ideas to be explored and more information to be learned about these snowy mountains and their behavior. Ski lifts must be checked regularly to see that they are in safe operating condition. Highway officials come to talk about taking more snow off the roads. In the evenings, there are slide talks to be given on skiing and avalanche control for the safety, education, and entertainment of guests at the lodge. Almost before one day ends, it is time to start another, but the snow rangers do their work with a sense of gratification, knowing they have served their fellow men well and contributed to their enjoyment of the mountain world. This is the snow ranger's job.

The man who works for the telephone company is equally proud of the part he has played in conquering the mountains with his communications system. Today you can talk to and from or over the mountains as though these masses were not even there. But telephone maintenance crews know about the mountains. Those who have been with the phone companies for more than twenty years remember meeting the mountains head-on in days when their lines were strung on poles through the heights just as they were in the lowlands. Keeping the lines strung, particularly in winter, was plaguing, and in some areas it seemed that they were down as much as they were up, despite the constant work of maintenance crews. "Walking the lines" to search out problems and make repairs was one of the jobs of the mountain telephone man, and in winter he made his treks wearing snowshoes. Sometimes the snow was high enough to bury the lines, sagging and snapping them with sheer weight, or often the culprit was a heavy coating of ice, a glittering spectacle of nature's jewel chest that came with thaw-and-freeze weather. Frequently the wind would whip the lines into tangles, or trees would topple over them. When the weather was worst, the lineman was needed most. From the Appalachians through the Rockies and the Sierras, wherever in the mountains there were enough people to need phone service, the lines went, and they climbed the passes—over even Loveland Pass at 10,000 feet in the Rockies—to get to the other side. Where the lines went, up and down the steep slopes, there were seasoned, rugged mountain men who chose as their work walking the lines to keep them in repair.

Times have changed the ways of mountain telephone men in most areas. They go to the mountains as before, but their work has been eased considerably by technology. The mountains are no longer the worry they were. In many places, the lines are buried. They snake through the valleys wherever pos-

Science in the Mountains: Tunnel of geophysical observatory of Colorado School of Mines gives access to seismic strainmeters, hermetically sealed in rock, which aid in forecasting quakes.

sible, but some still travel over the slopes. Paths are cut by superplows that can dig a three-foot-deep trench for burying a cable at the phenomenal speed of seventy-five feet per minute, ripping through the frozen dirt and rocks of the high places where work was once impossible. These are not single lines, of course; they are complex coaxial cables with as many as twenty tubes in a single heavily sheathed and insulated line. They have the capacity to transmit multiple communications without a mix-up.

Much communication over the mountains today is by an even more advanced system: microwave radio relay channels, requiring no lines at all. At intervals of fifteen to twenty-five miles are small buildings containing sophisticated radio relay equipment that operates automatically. Maintenance crews make regular service stops at these housings every two or three months. They go by snowcats or drop down from the sky in helicopters, and as soon as their inspection is completed, they are on their way quickly, leaving the mountains in brooding silence. Even their buildings are unobtrusive, melted into the landscape so that they seem an integral part of the mountains themselves. The service is better than ever, voices and other communications racing through and over the mountains with the speed of light, but men are still needed to work in the high places to keep it that way.

Many foresters, both men and women, are basically mountain people. Steep slopes are not convenient places for farming. In parts of Asia and other heavily populated areas of the mountain world, the slopes are benched to chisel out level parcels of land for growing crops, but where there is an abundance of land, only the lowlands are farmed. The mountains are more valuable for other purposes. Over a hundred million acres—more than half of the total—of government-owned forests in the United States are in mountain country, as is an almost equally large percentage of privately owned commercial forests. At the time of the discovery of North America, about half of the

243

continent was clad with forests. Today, nearly three centuries later, a third of the land is still wooded.

Foresters appreciate the importance of this vast acreage, and their work is to preserve it as a useful, renewable natural resource. From these forest lands, both government and private, comes the lumber used for building houses and other wood products. The harvests no longer exploit the woodlands—care is taken to assure a steady supply of trees for next year and in years to come. As trees are cut, they are replaced. On foot or in wheeled vehicles, as well as by balloon, helicopter, airplane, and skyline cables, the mountain foresters keep the slopes in growing green.

The value of the forests extends beyond the lumber itself, for much of the nation's water supply depends on these tree-clad lands, the thick-carpeted slopes and root networks beneath the surface acting like great sponges to hold back water and then feeding it slowly into the lowland aquifers for city water supplies, farmlands, and lakes and streams. New Yorkers' drinking water comes from a reservoir in the Catskill Mountains, more than a hundred miles from the city. Residents of Los Angeles draw from an aqueduct carrying water 250 miles, from the mountain headwaters of the Colorado River. Without their cloak of trees, slopes shed water like tin roofs—it rampages to sea level in devastating floods that wash away and impoverish the land.

The forests, too, are the home for much of the nation's fish and wildlife. Some have always been natives of the mountains; others have retreated to these wild places as a sanctuary. Whatever their origins, the mountains are now their home, and here the biologists, nature lovers, artists, and photographers go to find them for study or depiction in their natural habitats. For some species, management is necessary to keep populations healthy —such management includes controlled harvests, so that in select areas sportsmen also are an important part of the forest picture. Millions of vacationers turn to the forests strictly for the pleasure of being outdoors.

Almost everywhere in the world now, the mountains and their flora and fauna are recognized as natural treasures. Governments of dozens of countries have set aside vast areas of mountain terrain as parks and preserves, most of which can be visited to view and enjoy their splendors or to learn their coveted secrets. From truck drivers and loggers to professional foresters and biologists, from firefighters to office clerks and administrators—dedicated mountain people maintain these places. I know rangers who lead nature walks, give lectures, and man the visitor centers of national parks in Colorado, Wyoming, and Montana who would put up a fight if they were transferred to identical jobs in Oklahoma, Texas, or Florida. These are all people who love high country.

Real mountain people are indeed sentimentalists, sometimes even becoming rhapsodic in describing their mountain world.

Picture Credits

CHAPTER 1
10–11: Enrico Ferorelli. 12: Svat Macha, Amwest. 14–15: (top left) Enrico Ferorelli; (bottom left) Swiss National Tourist Office; (right) Klaus D. Francke, Peter Arnold. 16–17: Klaus D. Francke, Peter Arnold. 18–19: Erwin A. Bauer. 22: (top) Robert Burroughs; (bottom) Joy Spurr, Bruce Coleman. 23: Keith Gunnar, Bruce Coleman. 26–27: (left) R. Vroom, Bruce Coleman; (top right) Noel Habgood, Bruce Coleman; (bottom right) Lynn McLaren. 28–29: National Publicity Studios, New Zealand. 30–31: Werner H. Müller, Peter Arnold.

CHAPTER 2
34–35: Jacques Jangoux. 36: Swiss National Tourist Office. 38–39: (left) C. Haagner, Bruce Coleman; (top right) J. A. Cavanaugh, Bruce Coleman; (bottom right) Lee Lyon, Bruce Coleman. 42–43: (top left) Loren McIntyre, Woodfin Camp; (bottom left) Svat Macha, Amwest; (right) Björn Bolstead, Peter Arnold. 44: Ministry of Information and Tourism, Italy. 46–47: J. M. Bishop, Bruce Coleman. 48–49: Marilyn Silverstone, Magnum Photos. 50–51: (left) George H. Lowe III; (top right) Jacques Jangoux; (bottom right) B. Kielczynski, Bruce Coleman. 53: (top) Tass from Sovfoto; (bottom left) Ian Berry, Magnum Photos; (bottom right) Roland & Sabrina Michaud, Rapho/Photo Researchers. 54–55: C. D. Plage, Bruce Coleman. 58: W. E. Ruth, Bruce Coleman. 61: Svat Macha, Amwest. 62–63: (left) S. Jonasson, Bruce Coleman; (top right) Enrico Ferorelli; (bottom right) G. Shaller, Bruce Coleman. 65: Svat Macha, Amwest. 66–67: David Summer. 68: Svat Macha, Amwest. 69: Japan National Tourist Organization.

CHAPTER 3
70–71: C. D. Plage, Bruce Coleman. 72: Svat Macha, Amwest. 74–75: Enrico Ferorelli. 77: Ed Cooper. 78–79: (right) Anne LaBastille, Bruce Coleman. 82: Galen A. Rowell. 83: Robert Burroughs. 84–85: Frank J. Miller.

CHAPTER 4
86–87: Malcolm S. Kirk. 88: Keith Gunnar, Photo Researchers. 90–99: Gaston Rébuffat, Rapho/Photo Researchers. 103: (top) Author's Collection; (bottom left) Deane Hall; (bottom right) Foto/Frost. 104: Evelyn M. McElheny. 105–106: Ed Cooper. 109: Deane Hall. 110: Keith Gunnar, Photo Researchers. 114–115: Gaston Rébuffat, Rapho/Photo Researchers. 116: Keith Gunnar, Photo Researchers.

CHAPTER 5
118–119: Jacques Jangoux. 120: Australian National Tourist Office. 122–123: D. M. Durrance. 124–125: Peter Buckley. 127: George Holton. 128: French Government Tourist Office. 130–131: James Fain-Logan, Amwest. 134–135: Klaus D. Francke, Peter Arnold. 139: Noel Habgood, Bruce Coleman. 140: Ullal, Black Star. 141: Tass from Sovfoto. 142: (top) Candido Martinelli; (bottom) Enrico Ferorelli. 143: (top) Werner Müller, Peter Arnold; (bottom) Enrico Ferorelli.

CHAPTER 6
146–147: W. E. Ruth, Bruce Coleman. 148: Monkmeyer Press Photo Service. 151: Jeff Foott, Bruce Coleman. 152: Swiss National Tourist Office. 154–155: Keith Gunnar, Bruce Coleman. 157: UPI. 158: Swiss National Tourist Office. 161: Black Star. 162–163: (left) Southern Pacific R.R.; (right) Union Pacific R.R. 166–167: Rudolf Ludwig, Rapho/Photo Researchers. 168: Russ Kinne, Photo Researchers. 170–171: Paris Match/Pictorial Parade.

CHAPTER 7
174–175: Erwin A. Bauer. 176: National Park Service. 178–179: (top left) Bullaty Lomeo, Photo Researchers; (bottom left) Jacques Jangoux; (right) R. Vroom, Bruce Coleman. 181: Charles G. Summer, Jr., Amwest. 182: John S. Flannery, Bruce Coleman. 183: Peter Buckley. 185: (top) W. Franklin, Bruce Coleman; (bottom) G. Gualio, Bruce Coleman. 186: Keith Gunnar, Bruce Coleman. 187: (top left) Keith Gunnar, Bruce Coleman; (top right) Len Lee Rue IV, Bruce Coleman; (bottom) Thase Daniel. 190: (top) Mary M. Thesler, National Audubon Society/Photo Researchers; (bottom left) W. E. Ruth, Bruce Coleman; (bottom right) Bullaty Lomeo, Bruce Coleman. 191: Jacques Jangoux. 193: Swiss National Tourist Office. 194: G. Shaller, Bruce Coleman. 195: (top) G. Shaller, Bruce Coleman; (middle left) Robert Burroughs; (bottom left) H. Reinhard, Bruce Coleman; (bottom right) Erwin A. Bauer. 196–197: F. Erize, Bruce Coleman. 198–199: (left) Erwin A. Bauer; (top right) M. P. Kohl, Bruce Coleman; (middle) H. Reinhard, Bruce Coleman; (bottom right) Erwin A. Bauer. 202–203: (left) H. Reinhard, Bruce Coleman; (right) K. Fink, Bruce Coleman. 204: John S. Flannery, Bruce Coleman. 206–207: Keith Gunnar, Bruce Coleman. 209: Lee Lyon, Bruce Coleman. 210–211: (left) Erwin A. Bauer; (right) G. Shaller, Bruce Coleman.

CHAPTER 8
214–215: Enrico Ferorelli. 216: Australian National Tourist Office. 218: Peter Arnold. 219: J. Messerschmidt, Bruce Coleman. 222–223: Peter Arnold. 225: Australian National Tourist Office. 226: (top) Swiss National Tourist Office; (bottom, left & right) Australian National Tourist Office. 228: Canadian Government Travel Bureau. 229: Jerry Cooke. 230–231: Evelyn M. McElheny. 232: (top) Helmut Gritscher, Peter Arnold; (bottom) Paul Conklin, Monkmeyer Press Photo Service. 234–235: (top left) Evelyn M. McElheny; (middle left) Bill Browning; (bottom left) Erwin A. Bauer; (right) Bill Browning. 236: Author's Collection. 238–239: (left & bottom right) Erwin A. Bauer; (top right) Bill Browning. 240: Allyn L. Baum, Monkmeyer Press Photo Service. 243: Office of Public Information, Colorado School of Mining. 245: Erwin A. Bauer.

Index